Around the World

in 180 Days

by

Sherrie Payne

Around the World in 180 Days

Manufactured in the United States of America
Second Printing 2002

Published By

Apologia Educational Ministries, Inc.
Anderson, IN

Printed by

The C.J. Krehbiel Company
Cincinnati, OH

DEDICATION

To my children—

Geoff and Megan...for helping blaze the trail in our
multi-grade, one-room school adventure.

Kyle...who came up with the title for this book.

Cathy, Bethany, and David...who were the first to complete
this course and so willing to help when the decision was made to
produce this material for other homeschoolers.

To **Kris and Judy Wilcox** (The Book Peddler)...for their encouragement.

To **Jay and Kathleen Wile** (Apologia Educational Ministries)...for their help
and encouragement in publishing this book and designing the cover.

To my husband, **Rick**...because he never gives up on me.

And to my Heavenly Father...who so gently keeps on teaching me His lessons.

TABLE OF CONTENTS

GOALS FOR THIS STUDY

Taking each of the seven continents, one at a time, the following areas will be studied:

GEOGRAPHY (land forms, rivers, countries & cities, climate)
HISTORY (a brief overview of the history of each continent)
RELIGION (dominant religion/s of each continent; impact of Christianity)
CULTURE (government, economics, society, thought & learning, art)
KEY PEOPLE (missionaries, historical & political figures, artists, scientists)
CURRENT EVENTS/ISSUES (political, social, religious issues)

PURPOSE FOR STUDYING WORLD HISTORY & CULTURES

As you begin this history course, it is good to think for a moment about why we should even study the life and history of other countries. For the purpose of this multi-level history study guide, there are two major reasons the author had in mind when developing this course. The first reason is: "These things happened to them as examples and were written down as warnings for us..." *(I Cor. 10:32).* The second is summed up in the words of Jesus--"Therefore go and make disciples of all nations... teaching them to obey everything I have commanded you." *(Matt. 28:19-20).* In other words, as citizens of this country and of this world, and as Christians, we need to be aware of **what** *"things happened"* to **whom** and **why** so that we can be properly *"warned"*. And by gaining an understanding of another's culture, we can better learn how to share the gospel with any that we encounter as we *"go"* through life. The more we know and understand, the better our witness will be.

Another thing to think about: You may not even be considering leaving the United States as a missionary; however, it has become quite clear that today, God seems to be sending *"the world"* to our very doorstep. In some communities across the U.S., foreigners make up a very large part of its people. This is especially true on the West Coast, the southern Border States, and in many of the large cities. In towns with colleges or universities who usually have a certain amount of international students, there is a tremendous opportunity (responsibility?) to witness to the *"world"*! Let us, therefore, be challenged by this history course and "be diligent" to study so that you can "present yourself approved to God, a worker who does not need to be ashamed...." (II Tim. 2:15).

A Note from the Author about Multi-Grade Teaching

With six children and seventeen years of homeschooling behind me, I am beginning to feel fairly confident with teaching several grade levels at once. When I speak of several grade levels, I'm talking about all grades from kindergarten through high school. Many parents are fearful of teaching high school. I am very sorry whenever I encounter parents who send children to public schools solely out of fear of not being able to accomplish the task. I also wonder if families are aware of the blessing they are missing when the mom works with the younger children, but leaves the older teens to work with their grade level curriculum on their own. This isn't necessarily bad, but after teaching the old "one-room schoolhouse" way for so long, I am convinced that the high school years hold some of the best and most satisfying times for the entire family!

As your children reach their teen years and you are still teaching them at home, it is then that you can reap the benefits of all those years of training. In the home, there is not a chore that they are not able to do completely on their own. During school time, the discussions you can have with your teens are some of the most meaningful--whether it is about government or literature or science or the Bible. It is during the teen years that your teaching and training are the most solidly rooted. This does not take place by the eighth grade--it takes place all during those high school years! Don't miss out on this precious time by sending your older children away from you!

With the teens still in the homeschool, the younger children will have their world expanded by listening to the older ones as they discuss or question from their material. Obviously, the older children make perfect tutors for the younger ones, too.

And teaching all those grade levels together is not that hard. Granted, there are some subjects that have to be taught fairly systematically and individually, (i.e. the skill subjects of math and grammar), but the content subjects of history, science, and sometimes even literature can be taught to all the children at the same time. By using grade level textbooks and other resources, everyone can glean what they need at their particular level of ability.

I have also found that by keeping all my children together during school time, a learning beyond my planbook often takes place. For example, I will never forget the year my high schoolers and I were reading Shakespeare's *Macbeth* aloud together. That was the year I had literally a Kindergarten-to-Senior classroom. Since the reading was taking place orally, the younger ones could hear while they were working on their spelling, math, or other seatwork. Before too many days of reading had gone by, the upper elementary and junior high kids were asking if they could "choose a part" and join in the reading. At first I said that this was for high school, but finally consented to letting them join in--even though I figured they probably wouldn't really understand what they were reading. However, I drew the line at the second grader joining in. Finally, when the reading was over, I gave an assignment to the high schoolers to choose one of the speeches from the play to memorize and recite for the family. The younger ones in the group also chose to memorize a speech. But when my second grader announced that she planned to memorize Macbeth's speech--and did it!--that I realized how much she had comprehended just by listening to what was going on with her older siblings. At that time, I also realized what an advantage our little homeschool had over every *age-segregated* public or private school classroom in America. (By the way, our little second grader is now nineteen years old and can <u>still</u> recite Macbeth's speech!)

Our children are not limited to grade-level textbooks and a Board of Education time frame for what to learn and when to learn it. Although we have a planned course of study, our children are free to learn to whatever extent their minds will allow it. With older students in the classroom, I have found that the younger ones are able to handle much more than their traditional level of curriculum would offer them.

If you have not had the experience of teaching one subject to all your children together, this history/geography course is a great one to begin with. Around the World in 180 Days was developed one year when my high schoolers were scheduled for their world history course. Previously our world history study followed the typical course of study that began with ancient civilizations continuing through the Egyptians, Greeks, Romans. Then the Medieval Period was covered, followed by the Renaissance Period and the Reformation Era. Then came the Age of Discovery, the two World Wars, and the final chapters would cover Communism and the modern world. This was great, but what about the rest of the world? What about Africa? What about South America beyond the Line of Demarcation and Hernando Cortes? The only thing I knew about Australia was what I absorbed watching the *Five Mile Creek* videos. Antarctica was simply the South Pole to me. Our entire family's lack of knowledge of Asia and its countries and culture became apparent when we became friends with a young man from Malaysia who was attending the college in our community.

With all this running through my head, I thought, "Why not study world history **by the continent**? I know a good social studies course should cover not only history, but also geography and current events. Learning about the various cultures could be fun. As Christians, it would be useful to know what our churches are doing in the world on the mission field..." As all these thoughts went through my head, I also remembered a learning method that used the **"notebook approach"** where the learning was centered around the "4 Rs". The first "R" stood for **research**--the factual stage of learning with the answering of "what"-type questions. The second "R" stood for **reason** where the "how" and "why" questions were answered. The third "R" was the stage where the student would be asking himself "How does this study help me **relate** better to God and the world around me?" The fourth "R" represented the fact that the student would **record** or write down what he was learning.

Within that framework, we set out that year to study all seven continents. I had each student get a three-ring binder and insert seven tabs--each tab labeled with a different continent. We began with Africa. Starting with **geography**, they traced a map of Africa, using colored pencils and putting in as much detail as appropriate for their age. (If I had a very young student at that time, I would have just required an outline of the continent be traced, which is great small motor skills practice!) Then I typed up geography terms to identify and questions to answer which dealt with landforms, climate, and the flora (plants) and fauna (animals) of the continent. I had them define geographical terms beginning with something as simple as "jungle" and as unique as "wadi". They learned to identify special places on that continent--the highest mountain, the longest river, etc.

Next we began reading about the **history** that took place on that continent. At that point, we pulled out the grade-level history textbooks and went to the library for more books on our continent. [I need to make a special note here: I use the children's section of our public library for all my students--even if they are seniors in high school (unless they are doing in-depth research). I have found that even I learn from children's books, and using children's books lets the student spend more time on the material rather than muddling through the more adult/technical books on the subject just to get to the basic information.] Giving them questions to answer directed and focused their reading. This was a great way to teach the younger ones how to use the table of contents, chapter titles, and the index of a book to find information.

Next was the study of the **culture**. Studying the culture of a nation at any given point of time is a study of a people's way of life--the foods they eat, the education of their young, their clothing, the arts, crafts, music, what they do for entertainment, etc. The study of a culture also includes the study of a society's religion. We marked this as a separate section so that we could learn not only what the beliefs of a given group of people were, but also what place Christianity had in the various nations of a continent. We also tried to find out what success various missions had.

Every continent has **key people** who stand out in its history, so biographies were chosen to read. Different students chose different biographies. Sometimes I would have them write a summary of the person's life. Then we would make copies so that each student could have copies of their siblings' reports in their notebook too. We also read historical fiction books that had their setting somewhere on the continent. I tried to always be reading aloud to the children from a book pertaining to this continent as well (either a biography or historical fiction). Books written by an author from this continent were also on our list from which to choose.

All during the time we were focusing on a certain continent I had my children looking in the daily newspaper and listening to the news for **current events** relating to this area of the world. If something were in the newspaper, they would cut the article out, date it, and glue it to a sheet of paper that they added to their notebook.

As we progressed through our world studies that year, I saw how well this method worked for multi-grade schooling. For the older students, there were so many opportunities for more in-depth research and study. It taught the younger children how to use an atlas, a world almanac, as well as the encyclopedia. And best of all, we had fun with this project. We watched videos. We browsed through old magazines. We colored maps. And we found many, many fascinating books to read.

But best of all, we were studying something together--ALL together!

GOAL SETTING FOR GRADES K - 3/4

This multi-grade study works great with even the youngest students. Remember that the younger student really does not need to have structured social studies time each day. If they go through this material with their older siblings, they will be far ahead of schedule according to traditional curriculum scope and sequences. As you work with this age group of kindergarten through third or fourth graders, keep the following skills in mind. They are listed beginning with the simplest (kindergarten level) to the more complex (third and fourth grade levels):

The student should learn to...

- ☑ talk about what he sees and learns from pictures shown to him
- ☑ identify the globe as a model of the earth
- ☑ identify the globe as a model of the earth and distinguish between bodies of land and the oceans
- ☑ begin to understand what maps show and draw a simple map (i.e., a map of his room)
- ☑ identify where the United States is located on a globe or map
- ☑ become aware of the contribution of other cultures to our society (for example: ethnic foods)
- ☑ identify map and globe concepts of equator, hemisphere, continents, islands
- ☑ locate information in a newspaper
- ☑ locate requested information from books by using the title page, table of contents, chapter headings, and the index
- ☑ collect information and write a simple report
- ☑ interpret information from a graph
- ☑ make and read a time line
- ☑ understand how to use various kinds of maps and understand map keys

Your goals for them, other than the skills listed above, is to simply expose this age group to the world with its variety of people through the passage of history. There is an abundance of material for this age level in any library. The following homeschool curriculum and resource companies are a couple of my favorites who carry a large supply of books and/or resources you can purchase to add to your own home library. Just by browsing through their catalogs you will find many ideas for books to use not only with the younger students, but the older ones as well.

Geography Matters	**The Book Peddler**	**Sonlight Curriculum**
P.O. Box 92	P.O. Box 1960	8042 South Grant Way
Nancy, KY 42544	Elyria, OH 44036	Littleton, CO 80122

As you choose your books, plan which ones to read to coincide with what the older students are doing. When they are studying the geography, choose books which talk about the land. When culture is the topic, choose books with lots of pictures showing the people and what they are doing. Once you have your books, just sit down with them once or twice a week to read and look at the pictures. Leave time for answering questions and listening to comments. You'll be surprised what they pick up just listening to the older students.

HOW TO USE THIS STUDY GUIDE

Around the World in 180 Days contains a bound teacher's edition (with the answers) and one set of student pages appropriate for those in 4th or 5th grade through high school. Additional sets of student pages may be purchased for other students in the family. Some of the questions and activities have been labeled **UE, JH,** or **HS** (which stands for "upper elementary", "junior high", or "high school" grade-level questions or activities. See also the note at the end of this section.). Have your students insert his pages in a three-ring binder and place tab dividers between each of the continent sections. Label each tab with the name of the continent. If your youngest students also want to have a notebook, give them one with the same tab dividers. Purchase outline maps (or have an older sibling trace them) of the continents to color and label. Let them fill their notebooks with pictures from magazines, photocopied pictures from books, postcards, and so on. Look for pictures of the people, geographic features, animals, and plants of the area. Does your church support a missionary from this area? Write letters to them and insert their replies in the notebooks. Use what is available and what comes to your mind. Be creative!

You will need resource books. I like to use textbooks to get an overview of the material. My favorite grade-level textbooks are the seventh grade *World Studies* text from Bob Jones University Press (which I have used for students from sixth grade through high school). Bob Jones also has a sixth-grade text entitled *Heritage Studies* which would be good for the upper elementary students as well as a high school text. A Beka Book Publications has a good tenth grade text called *World History and Cultures,* a fifth-grade text that covers Old World history and geography, a sixth-grade text which covers New World history and geography (good for South and Central America work), and a seventh grade *History of the World.* When assigning work, check the table of contents in the texts and assign chapter or section readings pertaining to the topic in the study guide.

Your local library will be your best source for getting many of your books--especially for the primary, middle, and upper elementary students. Another resource that deserves a high recommendation is the **Link Homeschooler**, a free newsletter from Link International (A Ministry of The Voice of the Martyrs). This little newsletter features a country in each issue and gives information about its culture, language, and the condition for Christian workers. A family is introduced and suggestions given as to how you can communicate with them or help them. The unit-study-in-itself truly is a "link" between your homeschool and the world! Their address and phone number is:

Link International
A Ministry of Voice of the Martyrs
P. O. Box 433
Bartlesville, OK 74005-9935
(800) 747-0085

Most homeschooling families sooner or later wind up with a substantial home library. Depending on your school budget, several of the listed resources are "keepers". In other words, you may want to purchase them from the various homeschool curriculum companies. As well as the companies mentioned on page 11, books from Usborne and the Dorling/Kindersley companies are also excellent resources. Don't forget to check with other homeschooling families. Sometimes they may have the book you need and won't mind letting you borrow it.

The next thing to do is plan (approximately) the amount of time you want to spend on each continent. Then look through the questions and activities in the study guide. At that point you make the weekly (or daily) assignments. I like to use Mondays to introduce the material. I tell my children what we will be learning about during the week. I try to come up with questions for the purpose of exciting them about the upcoming study. For example, to my younger ones as we are getting ready to study Africa (or Asia), I might ask them if they knew that there were two kinds of elephants--an African elephant and an Asian elephant. Then I would ask them if they knew how to tell the difference. But I would not give them the answer, just telling them that they would soon find out. You can come up with questions similar to that by scanning the teacher's edition. If you learn something interesting, turn it into a "salting-the-oats" question (i.e., making them "thirsty" for knowledge).

The rest of the week I let my students work through the study guide. I give them help as they need it, by clarifying questions, helping locate answers, encouraging, and being interested in what they are learning. On Fridays I like to summarize what we've been learning throughout the week. At that time we go over the definitions and answers to the questions.

Notice that the name of this study guide is Around the World in 180 Days. It will be a fast trip to get through this in one school year. Take two years if you want. One mother told me she planned to make her children's notebooks on-going. As they came across information, they would just keep adding it to their notebooks!

If you want to take just a year, here is a suggested time frame:

Semester I		Semester II	
Africa	6 weeks	Asia	6-7 weeks
Australia	3-4 weeks	Europe	6-7 weeks
Antarctica	2 weeks	North America	4-5 weeks
South America	5-6 weeks		

Following this time schedule will lead you right into the next year's study of American history. Also, leaving Asia, Europe, and North America to study together during the second semester gives a framework for studying the two World Wars and modern history. (You might want to allow time to do a more in-depth study of the World Wars. There never seems to be enough time in a traditional world history or American history course to really learn the lessons of these two wars!)

Again, if you take only one school year to complete this unit, there is little time for in-depth study of a particular civilization. However, at the end of each section I have included suggested activities that will lead to a more intensive study of the continent. Some are more academic in nature; others are just for fun.

One more tip on multi-grade teaching: When evaluating your children's work, keep in mind the differences in ages and abilities. The high school student should be able to complete the notebook, do several of the suggested activities, and read a variety of books beyond his textbook. The junior high student should be able to answer most of the questions, do several of the activities (but not as in-depth), and read a variety of books. The upper elementary student should be able to answer at least half the study questions, do a few of the simpler activities, and still read at least one book or article for each continent. You know your child. He should be challenged, but not overwhelmed in his schoolwork. Judge accordingly.

RESOURCES

TEXTBOOKS

GRADE LEVEL	TITLE	AUTHOR/PUBLISHER
7-12	*Streams of Civilization*	Christian Liberty Press
7-12	*World Studies for Christian Schools*	Bob Jones Univ. Press
7-12	*History of the World in Christian Perspective*	A Beka Book
7-12	*World Geography in Christian Perspective*	A Beka Book
	A Glorious Age in Africa	Chu & Skinner

BOOKS OF INTEREST

4th & up	*The Slave Ship*	Sterne
4th & up	*Pyramid*	David Macaulay
4th & up	*The Pharaohs of Ancient Egypt*	Elizabeth Payne
5th & up	*Mara, Daughter of the Nile*	Eloise Jarvis MGraw
5th & up	*Journey to Jo'burg*	Naidoo
5th & up	*The Golden Goblet*	Eloise Jarvis McGraw
6th & up	*How I Found Livingstone*	Sir Henry Stanley
8th & up	*Cry, The Beloved Country*	Alan Paton
9th & up	*Heart of Darkness**	Joseph Conrad

*(Study guide available from Progeny Press)

MISSIONARIES TO READ ABOUT

Mary Slessor	C. T. Studd	Robert Moffat
David Livingston	Sir Henry M. Stanley	

OTHER PEOPLE YOU MAY WANT TO READ ABOUT

Cleopatra	Pharaoh Khufu (Cheops)
King Tut	Pharaoh Khafre

AFRICA: GEOGRAPHY

Use an atlas, encyclopedia, textbooks, and/or library books to find answers to the following questions.

IDENTIFY:

1. the large desert located in northern Africa - *the Sahara Desert*

2. the mountain range in northwestern Africa - *Atlas Mountains*

3. Africa's highest mountain peak - *Mt. Kilimanjaro in Tanzania*

4. Africa's largest lake - *Lake Victoria*

5. the world's longest river which is located in Africa - *Nile River*

6. Africa's second longest river - *Congo River*

DEFINE:

1. savanna - *large areas of grasslands   (Africa is more than two-fifths covered by savannas)*

2. plateau - *elevated area of flat land   (Africa is one large plateau broken by a few mountain ranges)*

3. steppe - *very dry grasslands, few trees, located near the deserts*

4. wadi - *dry riverbeds*

5. cataract (as along the Nile River) - *waterfalls or rapids*

6. delta - *a triangular deposit of soil formed at the mouth of some rivers   (the Nile River forms a delta)*

7. **tropical rain forest** - *vast forested areas in western and central Africa which receive more than 100 inches of rainfall each year*

8. **jungle** - *thick growth of plants found on the forest floor in tropical rain forests*

9. **Bedouins** - *nomadic Arabs living in desert areas who travel with their flocks following grazing areas (They are located on the Arabian peninsula as well as in the Sahara Desert.)*

10. **cape** - *a point of land which juts out into the water   (e.g., Africa's Cape of Good Hope)*

GEOGRAPHY QUESTIONS:

1. **[HS]**: Describe the topography of Egypt. Explain the difference between "upper Egypt" and "lower Egypt".

   [UE/JH]: Explain what is meant by "upper Egypt" and "lower Egypt".

   Egypt is mostly desert. A fertile valley extends along the Nile River which runs from the southern highlands to the north emptying into the Mediterranean Sea. The Sinai Peninsula also is a vast desert with mountains in the south. "Upper Egypt" is in the southern area of the country; it is __upriver__ on the Nile. "Lower Egypt" is the northern area or __downriver__ on the Nile. It is the opposite of usual "map language".

2. Describe the climate of Egypt.

   Egypt's climate is hot and dry with only two seasons--hot summers and mild winters.

3. Describe the climate (type of seasons) in the rest of Africa.

   Most of Africa has either a warm or hot climate. The humidity and rainfall vary greatly according to the region. The many desert areas receive little or no rain, but the coastal regions and the forests of the Congo Basin receive rain year around. Most of Africa, however, has one or two rainy seasons separated by dry seasons.

4. What is the source of the Nile River?   In what country is this lake located?

   Lake Victoria is the main source. It is located between the countries of Uganda, Tanzania, and Kenya.

5. What is the Great Rift Valley? How long is it?

   The Great Rift Valley is a series of long parallel cracks that form deep, steep-sided valleys. This region extends from the Red Sea coast through Ethiopia to Mozambique, running 4,500 miles in Africa.

6. In what country is Africa's highest mountain peak located?

   Tanzania

20

7. Where is "Timbuktu" located?   What is the history of this town and the meaning behind the phrase "as far away as Timbuktu"?

> *Timbuktu is located in the African nation of Mali on the Niger River. Hundreds of years ago, it was an important trade center that was visited by traders from as far away as Italy. In the 1300s it became a center for the arts and education. Schools and libraries were developed, bringing scholars from all over the world. The population was around 25,000 people at its peak. Today it is just a small town.*

8. List at least five of Africa's native animals. Also tell where each of these animals would be found (i.e., grasslands, jungles, etc.)

> *Grasslands: antelope, buffalo, giraffe, zebras, cheetahs, hyenas, jackals, leopards, lions, elephants, ostriches*
> *Rivers and Swamps: crocodiles, hippopotamus, flamingos, pelicans, storks*
> *Jungles (rain forests): chimpanzees, monkeys*
> *Madagascar: lemurs*

9. List at least three of Africa's native plant life.   Give the following information for each plant: 1) type of environment in which the plant is found
>   2) uses for the plant
>   3) any unusual description

> *Jungles (rain forests): oil palm, ebony, mahogany trees (hardwoods); okoume tree (softwood) used to make furniture*
> *Desert oasis: date palms, tamarisks, acacias*
> *Swamps: Mangrove trees (stand up on stilt-like roots)*

10. List several of Africa's natural resources.

> *Minerals: copper, diamonds, gold, petroleum*
> *Valuable forests*
> *Agriculture (produces most of world's cassava, cocoa beans, and yams)*

11. **[HS]** What was the country of Zimbabwe called before 1980?

> *Rhodesia*

12.   **[HS]**   What is a possible explanation for the Atlas Mountains, the Great Rift Valley, and the Mediterranean Sea? Where is the biblical reference to this catastrophic event?

> *There is evidence to suggest that the seven continents in the beginning were just one large continent (sometimes called "Pangaea"). Refer to Gen. 1:9,10. Then at some point, a cataclysmic event caused the continents to divide, even clashing together again, thus forming the Great Rift Valley and the Atlas Mountains. This could have happened during the Great Flood when the "fountains of the deep were opened up" (see Gen. 7:11) or shortly after the Flood in the days of Peleg (Gen. 10:25, I Chron. 1:19).*

22

MAP ACTIVITY.   Trace a map of the continent of Africa.   Label the following items.

Countries *(Capital Cities)*

___ Algeria *(Algiers)*
___ Angola *(Luanda)*
___ Benin *(Porto-Novo)*
___ Botswana *(Gaborone)*
___ Burkina Faso *(Ouagadougou)*
___ Burundi *(Bujumbura)*
___ Cabinda (belongs to Angola)
___ Cameroon *(Yaounde)*
___ Central African Republic *(Bangui)*
___ Cape Verde *(Praia)*
___ Chad *(Nidjamena)*
___ Congo *(Brazzaville)*
___ Djibouti *(Djibouti)*
___ Equatorial Guinea *(Malabo)*
___ Egypt *(Cairo)*
___ Ethiopia *(Addis Ababa)*
___ Gabon *(Libreville)*
___ The Gambia *(Banjul)*
___ Ghana *(Accra)*
___ Guinea-Bissau *(Bissau)*
___ Guinea *(Conakry)*
___ Kenya *(Nairobi)*
___ Ivory Coast *(Abidjan)*
___ Liberia *(Monrovia)*
___ Libya *(Tripoli)*
___ Mali *(Bamako)*
___ Malawi *(Lilongwe)*
___ Mauritania *(Nouakchott)*
___ Morocco *(Rabat*
___ Mozambique *(Maputo)*
___ Namibia *(Windhoek)*
___ Niger *(Niamey)*
___ Nigeria *(Lagos)*
___ Rwanda *(Kigali)*
___ Senegal *(Dakar)*
___ Sierra Leone *(Freetown)*
___ Somalia *(Mogadishu)*
___ South Africa *(Pretoria, Capetown)*
___ Sudan *(Khartoum)*
___ Swaziland *(Mbabane)*

Lakes, Rivers, Mountains, Seas

___ Lake Victoria
___ Lake Chad
___ Lake Nasser
___ Nile River
___ Congo River
___ Niger River
___ Red Sea
___ Mediterranean Sea
___ Gulf of Aden
___ Indian Ocean
___ Atlantic Ocean
___ Atlas Mountains

Islands

___ Madagascar *(Antananarivo)*
___ Canary Islands
___ Comoros Islands

Also label:

___ the Sinai Peninsula
___ The Great Rift Valley
___ The Cape of Good Hope
___ Aswan High Dam
___ Suez Canal

Countries *(Cities)* cont.

___ Tanzania *(Dar es Salaam)*
___ Togo *(Lome)*
___ Tunisia *(Tunis)*
___ Uganda *(Kampala)*
___ Zaire *(Kinshasa)*
___ Zambia *(Lusaka)*
___ Zimbabwe *(Harare)*

GEOGRAPHY ACTIVITY SUGGESTIONS: AFRICA

1. Memorize the capitals of several African countries. Set your own goal of how many and which ones (five countries, ten countries, all of them???). Mark the ones you choose on the Map Activity page (page 9) with an asterisk (*).

2. Mining Africa's mineral wealth accounts for about half of the continent's total exports. The world's largest producer of gold is the area of South Africa. Find out what other major minerals are mined on this continent and where the minerals are found. Create a key and plot this on your map of Africa.

3. ☜ ✍ The Sahara Desert is growing! Research this situation and find out what is being done to slow the progress. Write a short summary of what you find. (Suggestion: Check the Reader's Guide to Periodical Literature at your local library for magazine articles.)

4. The wild animals of Africa are world famous. Travel agencies book safaris to this mostly tropical land. Some go for the actual hunting and killing of the wild animals; others prefer doing their hunting with a camera. Suggested topics for a report are:

    [UE/JH]: Use your imagination! Pretend you are on a safari deep in the jungles of Africa. What animals do you see? What are they doing? ✍ Write a letter home to your family or a friend telling about your trip. [CREATIVE WRITING]
    NOTE: If enough research is done and enough detail is included, then this could also count for SCIENCE.

    [JH/HS]: ☜ ✍ Poaching continues to be a problem in Africa. Try to find out what is being done to limit this activity. How much of a problem is it? How much does it affect the country economically? Are some animals on the endangered species list because of poaching? Write or tell about your findings.
    [SOCIAL STUDIES/SCIENCE/SPEECH]

5. Study a product (land-use) map in an atlas. Notice how the map uses a symbol to represent the agricultural products or natural resources produced in a given area. Draw an outline map of Africa to make your own product map. Use your own symbols and make a key that explains what the symbols represent. Using colored pencils helps to make an attractive and readable map.

6. Study the time zones of the earth. Choose four different cities from this continent. Then calculate what time it is in those cities at the time you are doing this project.   [MATH]

Other Ideas/Notes:

AFRICA: HISTORY

ANCIENT HISTORY - EGYPT

Little is known about the early history of the continent of
Africa, yet one of the world's first great civilizations
developed in the northern part of this continent. The ancient
kingdom of Egypt arose along the banks of the great Nile River. Using your textbook,
atlas, library books, and encyclopedia, read about the remarkable ancient country of
Egypt. Then define the terms and answer the following questions.

TERMS:

1. Hieroglyphics - *ancient Egyptian form of writing*

2. Papyrus - *a plant which the Egyptians used to make baskets, boxes, mats, sandals, furniture, and paper*

3. Vizier - *a high official, second in command to the pharaoh*

4. Dynasty - *a ruling family*

5. Mummification - *the process of preserving dead bodies*

STUDY QUESTIONS:

1. What benefits did the Nile River give to the ancient Egyptians?

   Provided the soil and water needed to grow their food; provided a place for fishing; marshlands near the river were home to many waterfowl.

2. Why is Egypt often called "the Gift of the Nile"?

   Without the fertile soil deposited by the yearly flooding of the Nile, Egypt would be merely a wasteland.

3. What were the rulers of ancient Egypt called?

   The pharaoh was the head; the vizier was the second highest official.

4. What major biblical person was a vizier in Egypt?   *Joseph*

5. Why did the Egyptians build pyramids? What did this show about their religious beliefs?

   Pyramids were built as tombs to hold the dead. The tombs were filled with items that the deceased would need in another life--food, jewels, clothing, etc. The Egyptians believed in an afterlife.

6. Discuss the finding of the Rosetta Stone. (Why is it important? Who found this stone? What were they doing there?)

   The Rosetta Stone was discovered in 1799 by some men in Napoleon's army (which was invading Egypt). The writings were in three types of languages: Greek, demotic, and hieroglyphic. By using the Greek to translate the two ancient Egyptian writings, the hieroglyphic code was broken, thus allowing the translation of numerous other ancient Egyptian texts.

7. Egypt's ancient history is often referred to as having three eras -- the Old Kingdom, the Middle Kingdom, and the New Kingdom. Briefly describe each period.

   Old Kingdom: Consisted of the Upper Kingdom and the Lower Kingdom, which were united under the reign of Menes around 3100 B.C. This began the First Dynasty. The leaders of the Old Kingdom were considered divine rulers and were called <u>pharaohs.</u> The famous pyramids were built during this period as tombs for the pharaohs whose souls were believed to live in these tombs after their death. Hieroglyphics as a form of writing was developed in this era.

Middle Kingdom: *After a period of conflict and division lasting around 200 years, Egypt was again united under one pharaoh. Instead of building pyramid tombs, the focus was on rebuilding the country including a vast irrigation system. Foreign trade was important during this time. This was a time of prosperity and development. In the Old Kingdom, there were only the poor and the rich (the pharaoh and his noblemen). Originally, Egyptians believed that only the rich had a life after death. During the Middle Kingdom, a middle class developed, and the belief system eventually changed so that everyone would have a life after death, regardless of social class. Thus many more, though smaller, pyramid tombs were built during this time. The Middle Kingdom ended when the country was invaded by a fierce warring group from Arabia and Syria called the Hyksos.*

New Kingdom: *After approximately 100 years of foreign rule, the Egyptians were finally able to drive out the Hyksos from their land. After getting a taste of being able to conquer, the Egyptians turned their attention to conquering and invading other lands. There was military expansion, cultural growth, and rebuilding. Egypt became a great trade center for art and material goods. The New Kingdom ended with the rise of the Assyrian and Chaldean Empires.*

<u>Suggestions for Further Research on Egyptian History:</u>

1. ✏ ✍ Research the embalming technique the Egyptians used on their dead. Write a short summary of what you find.   (SCIENCE)

2. Find out how the ancient pyramids were built.
    - Give a "how-to" speech describing the procedure step-by-step. (SPEECH/COMPOSITION)
    - ✍Pretend you have been hired as the architect by the pharaoh and he wants a written report from you describing how you will get the job done. (COMPOSITION--CREATIVE WRITING)

3. ▤ Find out more about hieroglyphic writing. Make a chart of a few of the characters and include their definition.

4. ✏ ✍ There was one female pharaoh. Find out what you can about Queen Hatshepsut and summarize your findings in a report.

5. Read **Mara, Daughter of the Nile**. Choose a method below to report on the book.   (LITERATURE)
    - ✍ Describe Mara's personality and tell how she responded to various situations and problems she encountered.
    - ▤ Make a list of the facts you learned about ancient Egypt while reading this book.
    - ✍ Write a paragraph that describes the most exciting scene in the book.
    - ✏ Draw at least one picture from a scene in the story. (ART)
    - ✍ Write a "news brief" about the demise of Hatshepsut or Thutmose taking the throne of pharaoh.

6. ✏ ✍ King Tut is probably the one "mummy" we have all heard about. Research to find out when his tomb was found, who found it, why was he doing this search, and what he found (besides King Tut!). Where is "King Tut" now? Give your report orally.

<u>Other Ideas/Notes:</u>

ANCIENT & COLONIAL HISTORY - AFRICA'S INTERIOR

As already mentioned, little is known about the ancient history of most of the continent of Africa. However, the mystery began to unfold during the world's Age of Exploration (1500s); and Africa continued to reveal more of herself, even if reluctantly, during the Colonial Era. Use your resources to find out more by defining the following terms and answering the questions.

Terms:

1. Clan - *a group of people who are descended from a common ancestor*

2. Tribe - *two or more clans living together in a community*

3. Oral tradition - *poems, songs, or stories which are passed on by word of mouth from one generation to the next*

4. Imperialism - *the building of empires by a country*

5. Abolition - *doing away with or putting an end to (for example: slavery)*

6. Boers - *the Dutch who live in Africa*

7. Cannibalism - *the eating of human flesh*

8. Cartographer - *a person who draws maps*

STUDY QUESTIONS:

1. **[UE/JH]** Who was the head of the tribe in early African communities?

   the father

2. **[UE/JH]** What function or purpose did the "witch doctor" have in the tribe?

   He was the religious leader and his "power" was sought to cure both physical and spiritual problems.

3. **[UE/JH]** Why was the oral tradition so important to the early Africans?

   Before the 1800s, the Africans had no written languages. Therefore, for their history, traditions, and ancestry to be handed down to the next generation, it had to be told orally in a way that would be remembered. Children learned about their heritage from the "storyteller".

4. During the 19th century, serious exploration of the interior of Africa began to take place. What difficulties faced these explorers?

   Extreme heat and humidity, thick vegetation, unknown tropical diseases, hostility from the slave trade, wild animals, untrustworthy guides (who deserted them or led them to unfriendly tribes), rugged terrain

5. **[HS]** Because so many explorers died during this time, what nickname became attached to Africa?

   "White Man's Grave"

6. Which continent was responsible for the colonization of Africa?   *Europe*

7. Why were the Europeans interested in Africa? (What resources did this continent have? What did scientists find? What other kinds of information did they learn?)

   The African colonies held great wealth in their mineral reserves (gold, diamonds) as well as ivory, spices, and ebony. The Europeans were interested in finding out all they could about this unknown land. They followed rivers to their sources, took notes on the animal life and plant life, and studied the deserts and jungles.

8. **[HS]** What were some of the geographic features explored and charted during the period of exploration in Africa?

> *Victoria Falls, Lake Victoria, the Niger, Zambezi, and Congo Rivers, mountains, and deserts*

9. Who was probably Africa's greatest explorer? In what other role/s did he serve? When he died, what unusual thing was done with his body?

> *Dr. David Livingstone was also a doctor and a missionary. His body was buried in England, but his heart was buried in Africa by his African friends.*

10. Who was the discoverer of Victoria Falls? *Dr. Livingstone*

11. Who was Henry Stanley? (What did he do? What were his famous words? What impact did David Livingstone have on Stanley?)

> *Henry Stanley was a newspaper reporter. When Dr. Livingstone had not been heard from for several years, a newspaper editor sent Stanley in search of him. After a long search, Stanley found Livingstone deep in the heart of Africa by the shores of Lake Tanganyika. As Stanley approached Dr. Livingstone, he uttered the now famous greeting, "Dr. Livingstone, I presume". After Dr. Livingstone died, Stanley carried on his work in Africa.*

12. **[HS]** Describe the situation in Africa which led to the European slave trade. (How did they get the slaves? From whom were they gathered? What was the main reason for the growth in the slave trade? Where and why was there a "need" for slavery?)

> **[UE/JH]** a) Why were slaves taken from Africa? Where were they taken?
> b) Who sold the slaves to the European slavers? How did they get them and why did they take them?

> *Tribes were often at war with one another. Slaves were those from the captured tribe who were sold by the victor tribe. With the settlement of the Americas and the development of large plantations, manpower was needed to do the vast amount of work on these large farms. The slaves being offered in Africa seemed to be just the answer. A slave trade industry quickly developed with Britain, France, and Portugal being the main traders.*

13. Describe the conditions under which slaves were transported to their new location.

> *Slaves were bound together with chains or ropes to make the journey to the coast. Once on board they were chained to the ship. Usually the decks where they were kept had such low ceilings that the slaves were not able to stand up straight. Fresh air and exercise were rare.*

14. Where did the opposition to the slave trade begin?

> *Europe saw the cruelty of the slave trade and the drive to abolish it began first in England with other countries following the example.*

15. **[JH/HS]** Why was the African country of Liberia formed?.

> *The country of Liberia was formed in 1822 by a colonization society in the United States as a homeland for freed slaves. It was the first independent African republic. Monrovia, the country's capital city, was named after U.S. President James Monroe, who arranged for its founding. The name Liberia comes from the Latin phrase which means free land.*

16. Who was King Leopold II and what did he do that upset the other European nations?

> *King Leopold was the king of Belgium who claimed personal ownership of the Congo area (present day Zaire).*

17. What is the "Great Trek" and why did it take place?

> *After the British took over the Cape of Good Hope, which was formerly held by the Dutch, the Dutch (Boers) moved in great numbers northward out of the region.*

18. **[UE/JH]** Why was the Boer War fought? Who won? What new country was formed at the end of this war?

> *Many years after the Great Trek, gold and diamonds were discovered in the land occupied by the Boers. When the British wanted to control this area and take the wealth, the Boers defended their land. The British eventually won. The Union of South Africa was formed after this war.*

19. **[HS]** Before World War I, who controlled most of the African continent?

> *Various European powers (Great Britain, France, Italy, Portugal, Spain, Belgium, Germany)*

20. **[HS]**   What were some of the benefits of this foreign control to Africa?

> *This time of foreign control saw strong missionary work in Africa. Schools and colleges were founded. Roads, railroads, and hospitals were constructed. There was also an increase in the development of cities.*

21. **[HS]**   When did most of this foreign rule end?

> *during the 1950s and 1960s*

22. What are some of the problems and needs of modern-day Africa?

> *missionaries to continue teaching the Gospel; education to raise the low literacy rate*

Suggestions for Further Research on the History of Africa:

1. What is the "tsetse fly"? What impact did this fly have on Africa? (SCIENCE)

2. **[HS]** 📚 ✍ Research the practice of **apartheid** in South Africa. What is it? When did it end? What events contributed to its end? Has it been successful? Who is and what role did Nelson Mandela play in this situation?

3. **[UE/JH]** ✍ Write a paragraph about the good things that have come to Africa because of the Age of Exploration.

Other Ideas/Notes:

AFRICA: RELIGION

TERMS:

1. Polytheism - *believing in more than one god*

2. Monotheism - *believing in only one god*

3. **[HS]** Animism - *believing that natural objects and forces are inhabited by (usually malignant or evil) forces*

STUDY QUESTIONS:

1. **[HS]**   Describe the religion of ancient Egypt.   Were they polytheistic or monotheistic?   Who were the main god/s?

    [UE/JH]   Were the ancient Egyptians polytheistic or monotheistic? Who were some of the main gods that the ancient Egyptians worshipped?

    > *The Egyptians were polytheistic.   They were also humanists because they worshipped the man pharaoh and naturalists because they worshipped nature.*
    > *Main gods: Ra - chief god   Isis - protector of children*
    > *   Osiris - god of the underworld   Horus - the falcon god.*
    > *The pharaoh was considered a son of Horus, thus also a god.*

2. What did the ancient Egyptians believe happened to them after they died?

    > *They believed in an afterlife. In fact the Egyptians spent a lot of their time preparing for the afterlife. The rulers and other wealthy families built pyramids to house the bodies and other items they believed they would need to have with them to "enjoy" their afterlife. (The Egyptians called the soul that lived on their "Ka".)*

3. **[HS]**   Why did the Egyptians mummify their dead?

    > *The Egyptians believed that without a body they could not exist in the next world-- the world of the dead.*

4. Describe the religion of the typical African tribal community.

    There was a belief in a god who created the world and in lesser gods and spirits who ruled the affairs of the people. Sacrifices and rituals were performed to win the favor of these lesser gods in order to receive various blessings.

5. **[UE/JH]**   What did the Africans believe about their dead ancestors?

    They believed that they were still an active part of their family--that their spirits influenced them.

6. **[HS]**   What function or purpose did (does) the "witch doctor" have in the primitive tribes of Africa?

    [UE/HS]   a) Who was considered the tribal religious leader?
                          b) How did this religious leader "help" people?

    The witch doctor was the religious leader of the tribe. He had the job of curing the peoples' ills--whether problems with health or other problems such as bad fortune with life. He used his supposed magic powers diagnose the problem and prescribe the cure. Rituals, sacrifices, offerings could all be a part of this "cure".

7. Why were masks worn during religious ceremonies?

    Masks were made by the African craftsmen to represent faces of spirits or animals. During the religious ceremonies, the dancer wearing the mask supposedly became that spirit or animal. Each mask has a special purpose.

8. How is tribal art reflected in their religion?

    Objects or figures carved from wood, stone, or other material were believed to represent political or religious powers. Charms were also made for people to carry with them for their "good luck".

Suggestions for Further Research on the Religion of Africa:

1. ⚏ ✍ Read a biography of David Livingstone. Write a short report (one or two pages) which summarizes his life and work in Africa.

2. ⚏ ✍ Read a biography of Mary Slessor. Write a short report that summarizes her life and work in Africa.

3. **[HS]** ⚏ ✍ ▤ Research which denominations are currently the most active in evangelizing this continent. Make a poster or chart that records this information. What are the two top denominations as far as number of believers?

4. ▤ Write a letter to a missionary serving in Africa. Find out what you can about their life and work.

Other Ideas/Notes:

AFRICA: CULTURE

TERMS:

1. Swahili - *a mixture of Arabic, Persian, Indian, and native African languages*

STUDY QUESTIONS:

1. In the tribal African culture, what is the most important group of people?

   the family

2. Most African tribes practiced polygamy. Do you think it would be hard for the father/husband to keep peace in his family? Why or why not?

   Most likely there would be rivalry for the attention and favor of the father/husband between the different family groups.

3. **[HS]** How was music a part of an African's life? (When was music played or sung? What instruments were used?)

   [UE/JH] List some of the occasions where music would be a part of an African family's life.

   Music was an important part of the African tribal life. While working, playing, celebrating, or worshipping their gods, there would be singing or playing of instruments. Some instruments played might be drums, rattles, bells, or horns.

4. What were the "talking drums"? For what purposes were they used?

   Drums which could be tuned to different pitches. By playing these drums, tribes could "talk" or communicate with tribes in other villages miles away.

5. What other types of art did the Africans do?

   Africans also sculpted art objects from wood, stone, or other materials.

6. What were some of the reasons that a piece of art might be made?

    for religious ceremonies or "good luck" charms; to demonstrate wealth

7. List some ways that Africans obtained their food.

    hunting game, gathering fruits and nuts, herding, growing crops

<u>Suggestions for Further Research on the Culture of Africa:</u>

1. Read about one or more of the following areas of African culture. It may be the culture of the early tribes or the culture of a modern African nation. After reading, write or tell about your findings.

     ✎ African homes   ✎ African clothing

     ✎ African food   ✎ African schools

2. ✉ Write a letter to a missionary or other person you may know about working or serving in Africa. Ask them questions about life in Africa. (What foods do they eat? How do they travel? Where do the African children go to school? What kinds of clothes do they wear? What is their house like? etc.) Share your information with a display of pictures, articles, letters, postcards, etc.

3. ✎ Choose one African nation and research its government. Who is the leader of this nation? How is he elected? What other government offices or positions are there? Draw and color the nation's flag to put with your report.

4. Pick one of the primitive African tribes and research its culture. How do they live? How do they get their food? What is their religion like? What kind of houses do they have? What roles do the men and women have? Report your information in written form or orally.

<u>OTHER IDEAS/NOTES:</u>

AFRICA: CURRENT EVENTS

Use the space below to record the articles you have found or the news that you have heard during your study of Africa. Clip out the news articles and glue or paste them to a separate sheet of paper. Insert those pages after this page in your notebook.

Date of Newspaper or Radio/TV Broadcast	Name of Newspaper or News Station	Topic of News Item*
_____	_____	_____
_____	_____	_____
_____	_____	_____
_____	_____	_____
_____	_____	_____
_____	_____	_____
_____	_____	_____

* Examples: National currency, war, leadership, economics, government, environment, social issues, natural disasters (earthquakes, volcano eruptions)

~NOTES~

Australia

RESOURCES

Since Australia is not a typical part of the study of western civilization, most textbooks will not give much attention to this country. Your local library, however, will have many books which deal with the geography, history, and culture of Australia. There are also some interesting videos that can be used. (Our family enjoyed the "Five Mile Creek" video series.)

BOOKS OF INTEREST

5th up	*Walkabout*	Marshall
5th up	*Fight Against Albatross Two*	Colin Thiele
5th up	*Boy Alone*	Reginald Ottley
5th up	*The Roan Colt*	Reginald Ottley
5th up	*Rain Comes to Yamboorah*	Reginald Ottley
4th up	*Coral Reefs*	Johnson

AUSTRALIA: GEOGRAPHY

Use an atlas, encyclopedia, textbooks, and/or library books to find answers to the following questions.

IDENTIFY:

1. the world's largest coral reef located off the coast of Australia -

    The Great Barrier Reef

2. the world's largest single rock -

    Ayers Rock

3. the capital city of Australia -

    Canberra

DEFINE:

1. dune - *a sand hill formed by the wind*

2. artesian water - *water which is trapped underground with such great pressure that it gushes readily to the surface through any opening. Where artesian wells are dug, no pumps are needed.*

3. coral reef - *a ridge or shelf made up of limestone skeletons of certain sea animals. This shelf is located in tropical waters at or near the surface and is built up by the action of ocean waves.*

4. Aborigines - *the first or earliest inhabitants of a region (especially of Australia)*

5. strait - *a narrow channel of water which connects two larger bodies of water*

6. basin - *land that is drained by a river; a small or large depression in the surface of the land*

7. divide - *a ridge or other high place where the streams on one side flow in the opposite direction of the streams on the other side of the ridge.*

GEOGRAPHY QUESTIONS:

1. What is unique about Australia as a continent?

    Australia is not only a continent, it is a <u>nation</u>. It is also the smallest, flattest, driest of all the continents.

2. Why is Australia often called "the land down under"?

    Because it is in the Southern Hemisphere.

3. To what is Australia comparable in size?

    Australia is comparable in size to the continental United States.

4. What spectacular natural formation lies <u>off the northeastern coast</u> of Australia?

    The Great Barrier Reef

5. List the three main deserts located in Australia. Also tell in which part of the continent they are located.

    The Great Sandy Desert The Gibson Desert The Great Victorian Desert
    All three deserts are located in the central part of the Western Plateau region.

6. Besides the largest single rock in the world, what other interesting things could be found if you were to visit Ayers Rock?

    It contains small caves. Many of the cave walls are covered with rock paintings made by Aborigines.

7. What is found in the Great Artesian Basin and what is it used for?

    Artesian water is found in this basin. It is too salty for human use, but it is adequate for livestock. The water is also used for watering pastures.

8. What <u>can</u> be found in Lake Eyre? What <u>cannot</u> be found in Lake Eyre?

    Dinosaur bones <u>can</u> be found in Lake Eyre. Water <u>cannot</u> be found; it is a dry depression.

9. Does Australia have any mountains? If so, list them.

    The Great Dividing Range Australian Alps The Darling Range

10. How does Tasmania differ from the other Australian states?

   Tasmania is an island set apart from the continent itself.

11. How do the seasons of Australia compare to the seasons of countries in the Northern Hemisphere?

   The seasons are opposite. When it is winter in the Northern Hemisphere, it is summer in Australia and the rest of the southern hemisphere.

12. What are the seasons like in Australia?

   The northern third of Australia lies in the tropical zone; therefore, it is warm or hot the year round. It also has a dry season and a wet season. The rest of the continent has warm summers and mild or cool winters.

13. Which part of Australia receives the most rainfall?

   Queensland on the east coast is the wettest part of the continent. Other areas on the southern coast and Tasmania receive an even amount of rain over the year.

14. What is the Australian "outback"?

   This term refers to the interior country of the continent. This area is mostly open countryside with most of it used for grazing land. There are only a few settlements and mining towns in this vast area.

15. List four animals that are native to Australia.

   Kangaroo, koala, duck-billed platypus, wombat, wallabies, dingo, Tasmanian Devil....

16. List two native Australian birds.

   Emu, kookaburra, red-tailed cockatoo....

17. What two trees are native to Australia?

   Eucalyptus (gum) and Acacia (wattle) trees

<u>MAP ACTIVITY</u>.   Trace a map of the continent of Australia including its island state Tasmania.   Label the following items.

<u>States</u>	<u>*Capital Cities*</u>
___ New South Wales	___ *Sydney*
___ South Australia	___ *Adelaide*
___ Western Australia	___ *Perth*
___ Northern Territory	___ *Darwin*
___ Queensland	___ *Brisbane*
___ Victoria	___ *Melbourne*
___ Tasmania	___ *Hobart*

<u>Oceans, Seas, Rivers, Gulfs, Straits</u>

___ Indian Ocean	___ Pacific Ocean	___ Coral Sea
___ Murray River	___ Darling River	___ Tasman Sea
___ Gulf of Carpentaria	___ Bass Strait	

<u>Mountains, Deserts, Other Landmarks</u>

___ Great Sandy Desert	___ Gibson Desert
___ Great Victorian Desert	___ Australian Alps
___ Great Dividing Range	___ The Great Artesian Basin

<u>The national capital city:</u>

___ Canberra

GEOGRAPHY ACTIVITY SUGGESTIONS: **Australia**

1. Memorize the capitals of the seven Australian states.

2. Research to find out more about the Great Barrier Reef. What is <u>coral</u>?
    How large is this reef? What other sea life makes its home around the
    reef? ✍ Record your findings. (SCIENCE)

3. Research one animal found in Australia. ✍ Write or give a report that
    tells about this animal's environment--where it lives, what it eats. Also,
    give the natural enemies of this animal and how it protects itself. How are
    the young cared for? When are they considered an adult? Add any
    other interesting   information you find out. ✏ ✂ Draw or cut out a
    picture of this animal and add to your notebook.   (LIFE SCIENCE)

4. Read about Ayers Rock. What interpretations are given by evolutionists?
    by creationists? ✍ Record your findings.   (EARTH SCIENCE)

5. Study a product (land-use) map in an atlas. Notice how the map uses a
    symbol to represent the agricultural products or natural resources
    produced in a given area. Use the map you have already made or
    make another map to show your country's products. Use your own
    symbols and make a key that explains what the symbols represent. Using
    colored pencils helps to make an attractive and readable map.

Other Ideas/Notes:

AUSTRALIA: HISTORY

TERMS:

1. squatters - *early settlers who tried to get land illegally by occupying government land*

2. Anzacs - *an armed force called the Australian and New Zealand Army Corps formed during World War I to help the British*

STUDY QUESTIONS:

1. What are the Australian natives called?

    Aborigines

2. When and by whom was Australia "discovered"? What country did he represent?

    Australia was discovered in 1770 by James Cook of England.

3. What name did he give this new land (which he claimed for his mother country)?

    New South Wales

4. What event in American history directly affected the settling of Australia? In what way?

    The Revolutionary War. Before this war England had a practice of sending many of its convicted criminals to the colonies (especially to the colony of Georgia), which helped relieve the overcrowded condition in British jails. After the colonies won their independence from England, then the British decided to start a new prison colony in New South Wales (Australia). The first group of convicts arrived in Australia in January of 1788.

5. This new settlement eventually became what Australian city?

    Sydney

6. What event in 1851 attracted a new "rush" of settlers?

    Gold was discovered!

7. When did Australia become an independent nation?

    January 1, 1901

8. What type of government does Australia now have?

    a constitutional monarchy

9. What is the title of Australia's head of government?

    Prime Minister

10. Who is the official head of state?

    Queen Elizabeth II of Great Britain

11. What is Australia's national capital?

    Canberra

12. List the major exports of Australia.

    wool, wheat, sugar, beef
    (Australia is the world's largest producer and exporter of wool.)

<u>Suggestions for Further Research on</u> **Australian** <u>History:</u>

1. Read about the Australian Aborigines. How did they handle the incoming of the British settlers? What are their customs? Where do the Aborigines live today? What is their life like now? ✍ Give your findings in a report.

2. Draw a picture of the Australian flag. Explain its symbolism.

3. How does Australia's government differ from that of the United States? What is a <u>constitutional monarchy</u> form of government? What other nations have this type of system? Write a report or explain your answers orally to your family. [GOVERNMENT]

<u>Other Ideas/Notes:</u>

AUSTRALIA: RELIGION

Since Australia consists of two basic groups of people, the religions observed by the Australians also fall into two basic groups--the tribal beliefs of the Aborigines and various denominations of Christianity for those of British ancestry.

STUDY QUESTIONS:

1. Briefly describe the beliefs of the Aborigines who continue to practice their native religion.

    The Aborigines linked their religion and their land together. They believed that their ancestors of long ago had created the world in a period of time called the **Dreaming** *or* **Dreamtime**. *These ancestral beings never died but became a part of nature.*

2. List the most active Christian denominations of Australia in order of number of believers.

    1. The Anglican Church   (There are small Jewish and
    2. Roman Catholics   Muslim minorities.)
    3. Uniting Church
    4. Baptist   Eastern Orthodox   Lutheran

3. What is the *Uniting Church* of Australia?

    The uniting of the Methodist Church of Australia with the Congregationalist and Presbyterians. This took place in 1977.

<u>Suggestions for Further Research on the Religion of **Australia**:</u>

1. Find out if much missionary work is done in Australia. If so, by whom? What success are they having? Are there missionaries to the Aborigines?

<u>Other Ideas/Notes:</u>

AUSTRALIA: CULTURE

TERMS:

1. Boomerang - *a curved wooden club which, when thrown, returns to the thrower*

STUDY QUESTIONS:

1. What is the official language of Australia?

    English (with a mixture of British and Aborigine terms)

2. What is travel like for those who live in the outback?

    The outback has few paved roads, so automobile travel is limited, if not impossible. Ranchers and farmers who are fairly well-to-do usually own light airplanes. There is a highway that circles the continent that truckers use. They pull several semis at once and are called "road trains".

3. How do children who live in the outback receive their education?

    Each Australian state operates a correspondence school for families living in remote areas. They also operate "schools of the air" which allows students to communicate with a teacher by two-way radio.

<u>Suggestions for Further Research on the Culture of **Australia:**</u>

1. Read to find out some of the words unique to the Australian language. Make a list of ten or more of these words and their English (American) equivalent.

2. With the arrival of the OUTBACK® restaurants in our larger cities, we can get a taste of traditional Australian cooking. If you can't visit the restaurant, then try to find out what type of foods are typical of Australia's kitchens. Then make out a menu and describe each dish. ✍ Tell how the food was prepared (in an oven; on the "barby") as well as the main ingredients.

<u>OTHER IDEAS/NOTES:</u>

AUSTRALIA: CURRENT EVENTS

Use the space below to record the articles you have found or the news that you have heard during your study of Australia. Clip out the news articles and glue or paste them to a separate sheet of paper. Insert those pages after this page in your notebook.

Date of Newspaper or Radio/TV Broadcast	Name of Newspaper or News Station	Topic of News Item*
_____	_____	_____
_____	_____	_____
_____	_____	_____
_____	_____	_____
_____	_____	_____
_____	_____	_____
_____	_____	_____

* Examples: National currency, war, leadership, economics, government, environment, social issues, natural disasters (earthquakes, volcano eruptions)

~Notes~

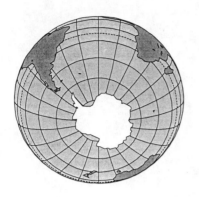

ANTARCTICA

RESOURCES

Obviously, Antarctica is not a big topic of study in a history curriculum. Most textbooks will give only a passing mention to this continent. *National Geographic* and other magazines of this type are probably the best resource. There are also some interesting videos that can be used. Check your library.

Video: "The Big Ice"

PEOPLE YOU MAY WANT TO READ ABOUT

Richard E. Byrd   Robert F. Scott   Roald Amundsen

ANTARCTICA: GEOGRAPHY

Use an atlas, encyclopedia, textbooks, and/or library books to find answers to the following questions.

DEFINE:

1. ice shelf - *a platform of ice that rests on the sea*

2. ice floes - *sheets of ice that have frozen over the winter in the ocean and in the summer breaks into pieces*

3. icebergs - *a large floating mass of ice which has broken off from a glacier*

4. krill - *small, shrimp-like creatures abundant in the ocean and used for food by other polar animals*

5. calving - *when pieces of glaciers break off (forming icebergs)*

GEOGRAPHY QUESTIONS:

1. To what can Antarctica be compared for size?

    Antarctica is about the size of North American and Mexico combined. It is larger than Europe or Australia.

2. At which pole is Antarctica located?　　　　*The South Pole*

3. Describe the climate of this continent. What is the range in temperature from the coldest to the warmest?

    Antarctica's inland plateau is cold and dry. It receives about two inches of rainfall each year. The coastal areas are slightly warmer and moister, receiving approximately twenty-four inches of rain per year. Winter (May through August) sees temperatures ranging from -40° to -94°(F) in the interior and a range from -5° to -22°(F) on the coast. Summer temperatures (December through February) range from +5° to -30°(F) in the interior and can reach 32°(F) on the coast. The winds also add to the continent's coldness by averaging over 40 miles per hour.

4. Are there any mountains on Antarctica?　　　　*yes*

    What are they called?

    The Transantarctic Mountains　　Prince Charles Mountains　　Ellsworth Mountains

5. Give the names of some of the ice shelves that are part of this continent.

    Ross Ice Shelf　　　　Larsen Ice Shelf
    Filchner Ice Shelf　　Shackleton Ice Shelf

6. Is the ice on Antarctica from salt water or fresh water?

    fresh water

7. Does this continent have any cities or towns?

    no

8. Do people visit or work on Antarctica?

    yes

9. Where do these people stay and what do they do?

    There are approximately 50 scientific stations set up for research.

10. List the natural resources of Antarctica.

    fresh water (frozen!), oil, gold, copper, coal in small quantities

11. What animals can be found on Antarctica?

    *whales, penguins, seals, several kinds of birds--albatrosses, gulls,
    petrels, terns*

12. Can any vegetation be found there?   *yes*

    If so, what kind?

    *Mosses, algae, lichens, grass can often be found on sunny slopes or on the coastal
    areas where it gets a little warmer.*

<u>MAP ACTIVITY.</u> Trace a map of the continent of Antarctica. Label the following items.

Stations

____ Little America (USA)

____ Scott   (New Zealand)

____ McMurdo   (USA)

____ Amundsen-Scott   (USA)

____ Wilkes   (Australia)

____ Vostok   (Russia)

Areas

____ Marie Byrd Land

____ Victoria Land

____ Queen Maud Land

____ Antarctic Peninsula

____ Ross Ice Shelf

____ Ronne Ice Shelf

Oceans, Seas, Rivers

____ Pacific Ocean

____ Atlantic Ocean

____ Weddell Sea

____ Indian Ocean

____ Amundsen Sea

Other Landmarks

____ Transantarctic Mountains

____ Arctic Circle

____ South Pole

GEOGRAPHY ACTIVITY SUGGESTIONS: **Antarctica**

1. Try to find the meaning of the name "Antarctica". Why was it given this name?

2. ✇ Research the tiny krill. Why is this little sea creature so important to the survival of every other animal that makes Antarctica its home.

Other Ideas/Notes:

Antarctica: HISTORY

<u>STUDY QUESTIONS:</u>

1. List three early explorers and the countries they were from who were searching for this "unknown last continent"?   (They may not have actually sighted land.)

    1772 - Capt. James Cook, an English navigator began his search for the southern continent.
    1841 - John Biscoe, an English whaler was first to spot land in East Antarctica.
    1837 - Lt. Jules d'Urville of France was sent by his King to claim southern lands.
       Lt. Charles Wilkes of the US Navy explored the coastal regions of Antarctica.
    Others: James Clark Ross of England; Henry Johan Bull of Norway

2. Who were the two men who lead the "Great Race" to the South Pole? What year did this take place?

    In 1909 explorers had reached the North Pole. In 1910, Robert Falcon Scott of England and Roald Amundsen of Norway each hoped to gain the honor of being the first to reach the South Pole.

3. Briefly describe this race. Who won and by how long?

    Although Scott and Amundsen never met, they were both aware of each other and the common goal of being the first to arrive at the South Pole. Amundsen, with four assistants and fifty-two Eskimo dogs, began his trek across the ice on October 19, 1911. Scott, with fifteen men, motorized sleds, ponies, and dogs, began his walk nearly two weeks later on November 1, 1911. Amundsen arrived at the South Pole on December 14, 1911 with only eleven dogs but all five men were in good health. He left the Norwegian flag and a note for Scott at the pole. Scott's group reached the pole on January 17, 1912.

4. Who was the first man to fly over the South Pole?   What country was he from?

    U. S. Navy officer Richard E. Byrd in November of 1929

5. Who has claim or control of this continent?

    No one, technically

6. When was this determined?   What was this agreement called?

    in 1959 with the Antarctic Treaty

7. Why were stations set up in Antarctica in the late 1950s?

    for scientific research

8. What was the international organization that led to these stations being established? How many countries first participated?

    The **<u>International Geophysical Year</u>** (**IGY**) *was a program established so that scientists could carry out research and share their findings with each other. This took place from July 1, 1957 until December 31, 1958. During this time 12 countries established 50 research stations on Antarctica and nearby islands. Studies were done in the areas of weather, earthquakes, gravity, oceans, magnetism, as well as measuring the thickness of the icecap and the general lay of the land.*

9. List the three main American stations located on Antarctica.

    Little America   *McMurdo*   *Amundsen-Scott*

10. What kinds of fossils have been found on this continent?

    tree trunks, ferns, dinosaur bones

11. What are some of today's concerns regarding Antarctica?

    There is concern from all the continents that this area could become polluted, exploited, or used for self-gain.

<u>Suggestions for Further Research on ANTARCTICA's History:</u>

1. 📖 ✍ Read one magazine article that deals with Antarctica. Summarize the article. Include the name and date of the magazine with your report.

2. 📖 ✍ Read about the "Great Race" to the South Pole. Compare the number of assistants each man took with him, the number of animals used to pull the   sleds, the types of provisions carried. Find out whether both teams made it safely back to their starting point. Give an oral or written report on your findings. Or, 📄 make a poster that compares the two teams.

3. 📖 ✍ There is much in the news about the thinning of the ozone layer located over Antarctica. Is there really a "hole" in the ozone layer? What are some of the theories presented by scientists today? Report your findings.

<u>Other Ideas/Notes:</u>

Antarctica: CURRENT EVENTS

Use the space below to record the articles you have found or the news that you have heard during your study of Antarctica. Clip out the news articles and glue or paste them to a separate sheet of paper. Insert those pages after this page in your notebook.

Date of Newspaper or Radio/TV Broadcast	Name of Newspaper or News Station	Topic of News Item*
_____	_____	_____
_____	_____	_____
_____	_____	_____
_____	_____	_____
_____	_____	_____
_____	_____	_____
_____	_____	_____

* Examples: National currency, war, leadership, economics, government, environment, social issues, natural disasters (earthquakes, volcano eruptions)

~notes~

SOUTH AMERICA

RESOURCES

TEXTBOOKS

GRADE LEVEL	TITLE	AUTHOR/ PUBLISHER
4-6	*New World History and Geography*	A Beka Book
9-12	*History of the World* in Christian Perspective	A Beka Book
7-12	*World Studies for Christian Schools*	Bob Jones Univ. Press
7-12	*World Geography in Christian Perspective*	A Beka Book

BOOKS OF INTEREST/READERS

4-6	*The Secret of the Andes*	Clark
4th up	*Chucaro; Wild Pony of the Pampa*	Kalnay
4th up	*Out on the Pampas*	G. A. Henty
5th up	*Bruchko*	Bruce Olson
5th up	*Walk the World's Rim*	Baker
5th up	*The Panama Canal*	Stein
5th up	*Through Gates of Splendor*	Elliott
6th up	*Kon-Tiki*	Heyerdahl

OTHER PEOPLE YOU MAY WANT TO READ ABOUT

Simon Bolivar   Jose de San Martin

SOUTH AMERICA: GEOGRAPHY

Use an atlas, encyclopedia, textbooks, and/or library books to find answers to the following questions.

IDENTIFY:

1. the mountain range which runs along the western coast of South America -

    Andes Mountains

2. the tallest mountain in the western hemisphere and where it's located -

    Aconcagua, Located in Argentina

3. the water falls which has the longest drop of any in the world and where it is located -

    Angel Falls, located in Venezuela

DEFINE:

1. isthmus - *a narrow strip of land that connects two larger bodies of land*

2. mountain range - *a row of connected mountains*

3. island - *a body of land (smaller than a continent) that is completely surrounded by water*

4. rain forest - *a tropical forest in an area where there is an exceptionally high amount of yearly rainfall*

5. sea - *a body of salt water (smaller than an ocean)*

6. pampas - *huge, treeless plains (especially in Argentina)*

GEOGRAPHY QUESTIONS:

1. List the areas (not countries) that are included in the South American continent.

   Central America, South America, and the Falkland Islands

2. In which hemisphere is South America located?

   the Southern Hemisphere

3. South America is the fourth largest continent. What are the three larger continents?

   Asia   Africa   North America

4. The world's largest rain forest is located on this continent. Where is this forest located?

   in the Amazon River Basin in the country of Brazil

5. What is the name of the desert located in northern Chile?

   Atacama Desert

6. Which three South American countries are largely made up of rolling grasslands?

   Argentina, Venezuela, and Colombia

7. The isthmus of Panama links Central America with South America at what country?

   Colombia

8. List several of South America's native animals and describe any unusual characteristics as well as its natural habitat.

   The <u>capybara</u> is the world's largest rodent and lives in the Amazon River Basin. The <u>sloth</u> is one of the slowest mammals and lives in the trees of the rain forest. The Amazon River is home to one of the world's longest snakes--the <u>anaconda,</u> as well as the <u>piranha</u> fish (a school of piranhas may attack a much larger animal, eating all the flesh and leaving only the bones). In the pampas of Argentina live the large <u>rhea</u>, which resembles an ostrich. The Andes Mountains are home to the <u>alpaca</u> (which produce fine wool) and the <u>llama</u> (a pack animal).

9. List several plants native to South America.

> *orchids, the rubber tree, cacao tree, pineapple plant, carnuba palm*

10. What major islands or island groups are part of South America?

> *Calapagos Islands   Tierra del Fuego   Falkland Islands*

MAP ACTIVITY. Trace a map of the continent of Latin (South) America. Label the following items.

Countries & Islands *(Capital Cities)*

___ Colombia *(Bogota)*

___ Argentina *(Buenos Aires)*

___ Guyana *(Georgetown)*

___ Suriname *(Paramaribo)*

___ Brazil *(Brasilia* - also show: *Sao Paulo, Rio de Janeiro)*

___ Bolivia *(La Paz)*

___ Uruguay *(Montevideo)*

___ Panama *(Panama)*

___ Nicaragua *(Managua)*

___ Guatemala *(Guatemala)*

___ Belize *(Belmopan)*

___ Cuba *(Havana)*

___ Haiti *(Port au Prince)*

___ Dominican Republic *(Santo Domingo)*

___ Grand Cayman

___ Martinique

___ Guadeloupe

___ Netherlands Antilles

___ Saint Vincent

___ Antigua

___ Tierra del Fuego

___ Peru *(Lima)*

___ Ecuador *(Quito)*

___ Venezuela *(Caracas)*

___ French Guiana *(Cayenne)*

___ Panama *(Panama)*

___ Paraguay *(Asuncion)*

___ Chile *(Santiago)*

___ Costa Rica *(San Jose)*

___ Honduras *(Tegucigalpa)*

___ El Salvador *(San Salvador)*

___ Mexico *(Mexico D. F.)*

___ Bahamas *(Nassau)*

___ Jamaica *(Kingston)*

___ Puerto Rico *(San Juan)*

___ Dominica

___ Barbados

___ Saint Lucia

___ St. Kitts

___ Grenada

___ Galapagos Islands

___ Cape Horn

Oceans, Seas, Rivers, Gulfs, Straits

___ Caribbean Sea   ___ Pacific Ocean   ___ Atlantic Ocean

___ Gulf of Mexico   ___ Strait of Magellan   ___ Panama Canal

___ Amazon River   ___ Orinoco River   ___ Uruguay River

___ Sao Francisco River

Mountains, Deserts, Other Landmarks

___ Andes Mountains   ___ Atacama Desert

___ Sierra Madres Oriental Mountains   ___ Baja California

___ Sierra Madres Occidental Mountains   ___ the equator

___ Tropic of Cancer   ___ Tropic of Capricorn

<u>GEOGRAPHY ACTIVITY SUGGESTIONS:</u> **SOUTH AMERICA**:

1. Memorize the capitals of several or all of the South American countries.

2. ☙ ✍ Research to find out more about the rain forests of South America. What is the economic importance of this area? Record your findings. (SCIENCE)

3. ☙ ✍ Research one animal found in South America. Write or give a report that tells about this animal's environment--where it lives, what it eats. Also, give the natural enemies of this animal and how it protects itself. How are the young cared for? When are they considered an adult? Add any other interesting information you find out. ✍ ✂ Draw or cut out a picture of this animal and add to your notebook. (LIFE SCIENCE)

4. Study a product (land-use) map in an atlas. Notice how the map uses a symbol to represent the agricultural products or natural resources produced in a given area. Draw an outline map of South American and then use your own symbols to make a key that explains what the symbols represent. Using colored pencils helps to make an attractive and readable map.

<u>Other Ideas/Notes:</u>

SOUTH AMERICA: HISTORY

TERMS:

1. Iberians - *Spaniards or Portuguese*

2. viceroys - *Spanish rulers appointed by the King*

3. Creoles - *persons of Spanish descent born in America*

4. Caudillos - *military leaders that overthrew the government*

5. hacienda - *a large farm, ranch, or country estate*

6. mestizos - *descendants of mixed Indian and European ancestry*

7. mulattos - *descendants of mixed Black and European ancestry*

8. conquistador - *a Spanish adventurer with small, but well-equipped army*

STUDY QUESTIONS:

1. The word "Indians" refers to what group of people in South America?

    the native or original inhabitants of the continent

2. What were the three main Indian groups on this continent before the European explorers arrived?

    the Mayan, the Aztecs, and the Incas

3. Which nation was responsible for conquering the great Indian nations of South America?

    Spain

4. Who was the Inca leader at the time of the conquest by the Europeans?

    Atahualpa

5. Who led the conquering of the Inca Indians?

    Francisco Pizarro

6. Which tribe controlled the Valley of Mexico and the area surrounding it?

    the Aztecs

7. What was the name of the Aztec capital?   *Tenochtitlan*

    What is the present-day name for this area?   *Mexico City*

8. Who was the leader of the Aztecs when the Europeans first arrived in this area?

    Montezuma II

9. Which European leader conquered the Aztecs?

    Hernando Cortés

10. Besides his own men, who also helped in him in the conquering?

    He was helped by the surrounding Indian tribes who had been conquered by the Aztecs and resented their heavy taxes.

11. Why did the Aztecs not oppose the European conquerors?

The Aztecs had a legend that their god (who was a white man) had sailed across the ocean and that someday he would return. When Cortés and his men appeared, they believed that this was their god returning.

12. What group of Indians in southern Chile were able to resist being conquered for over 300 years?

the Araucanian Indians

13. Besides being killed in battles, what was another reason for the decline in the Indian population after European colonists arrived in Latin America?

The European colonists brought diseases with them that the Indians did not have an immunity to. The Indians also died from the harsh treatment suffered at the hands of the settlers.

14. Of the four major European countries that had the greatest number of people settling in the New World, which two of these countries focused mostly on the southern continent?

Spain and Portugal

15. Why is this area often referred to as "Latin America"?

All the languages spoken on this continent are derivatives of Latin.

16. What was one major reason Europeans came to the New World?

to search for gold, silver, iron ore, precious gems

17. What did South America have more of than North America?

silver and gold

18. Which church group took hold in Latin America?

the Roman Catholic Church

19. Which area in South America did the Portuguese government control?

Brazil

20. Why was an imaginary line drawn which ran north and south through South America?   What was this line called?

   The Line of Demarcation was drawn up after the discovery of the New World. To prevent disputes between Spain and Portugal over who could claim the lands in the southern continent, Pope Alexander VI said that Spain could claim lands west of this line and Portugal could claim the lands to the east. Two years later in 1494, Portugal claimed that Spain had a bigger section, so the line was moved farther west. Portugal then settled the large area that is now the country of Brazil. Spain settled in the rest of the continent.

21. Who were the two men who led revolutions to gain independence for South America from its European rulers?

   Jose de San Martin   *Simon Bolivar*

<u>Suggestions for Further Research on SOUTH AMERICAN History:</u>

1. ⬱ Read about life on a hacienda during the settlement period of South America. How did this compare or contrast with life in a medieval European castle.

2. Describe the problems that the Latin American countries faced as they tried to rule themselves. How has this carried through even until today?

3. Make a time line of the important historical events of this continent. Some points to include would be:
    - Peak of Mayan Indian civilization
    - Peak of Aztec Indians empire
    - Peak of Inca Indian empire
    - Christopher Columbus--first European to reach Latin America
    - Magellan rounds the tip of South America through the strait that now bears his name
    - Spanish conquest of the major Indian civilizations completed
    - Most Latin American colonies gain their independence

4. What is a **bola**? How and for what purpose was this used by the Indians?

5. ⬱ ✍ The United States was not the only nation that had to fight to gain its freedom from European control after the New World was discovered. Read about the fight for freedom of Mexico, the other Central American countries, Brazil, or the other South American countries. Choose one area and write two to four paragraphs which briefly tell when the independence was gained, who led the fight, and how the independence was finally obtained.

92

Other Ideas/Notes:

South America: RELIGION

STUDY QUESTIONS:

1. **[HS]** The encyclopedia says that most Latin Americans are "Christians". What do they mean by that statement?

   Latin America was settled by the nations of Spain and Portugal, which had Roman Catholicism as their state religion. In fact, the settlers were commanded by their government to convert the native Indians to Catholicism. To this day some nations officially still support the Roman Catholic Church, although the laws of all the nations guarantee freedom of worship. Technically, "most" Latin Americans are Christians, but the number who actually practice and live the Christian life varies greatly. Because of the work of missionaries, the number of Protestant and evangelical Christians is growing today.

2. **[UE/JH]** Which denomination or church do the majority of Latin Americans belong to?

   The Roman Catholic Church

3. **[UE/JH]** Do the people of Latin America have the freedom to worship as they choose?

   Yes

4. **[UE/JH]** Do some governments in Latin America officially support a particular church? If so, which one?

   Yes. The Roman Catholic Church

5. What percentage of the people are considered to be Protestant?

   a little over 5%

6. Name some of the most active Protestant denominations in Latin America.

   Baptists, Methodists, Pentecostals, Episcopalians, Lutherans

7. Which two church groups have the fastest growing membership today in Latin America?

   the Pentecostal Churches and the Mormons (Church of Jesus Christ of Latter-day Saints)

Suggestions for Further Research on the Religion of SOUTH AMERICA:

1. ▣ Many churches support missionaries who are working in Latin America. Try to make contact with one and ask them about their work, such as: What is your biggest challenge in reaching these people?   Are the people receptive to your message? What types of outreach seem to work best? Do you have churches in villages or are they in large cities?

2. The Mormons are one of the largest "churches" in Latin America. Research to find out why this church seems to have a foothold in this area.

Other Ideas/Notes:

SOUTH AMERICA: CULTURE

TERMS:

1. poncho - *a blanket with a slit in the middle for the head; worn by the people in cooler mountain villages as a coat*

2. gauchos - *cowboys of Argentina and Uruguay*

3. tortilla - *a thin pancake made from corn flour*

4. hacienda - *a large plantation or farm*

5. fiesta - *a festival*

STUDY QUESTIONS:

1. Describe some of the typical foods that would be eaten in South America.

    Beans, rice, and tortillas make up the staple diet. (Spicy foods are favored in many of the countries, but not all of them as commonly believed.)

2. What forms of recreation are enjoyed by the people of South America?

    Soccer is probably the most popular sport. (In the 1960s the world's greatest soccer player, Pele, came from Brazil.) Cricket and bullfights are also traditional favorites.

3. Discuss the educational system of South America. Are most Latin Americans literate?

    The literacy rate has been very low in many parts of Latin America. However, governments in several of the countries are focusing on education. Programs have even been started to help illiterate adults learn to read and write. There are still problems with getting and keeping children in school (especially a problem in the rural areas.)

Suggestions for Further Research on the Culture of SOUTH AMERICA:

1. ♫ What are the traditional instruments used in Latin American music? What are "mariachis"? Try to find where the following music styles originated from: *samba, calypso, bossa nova.*

2. Latin American dancing is also well known. Some steps that originated in Latin America are taught in North American ballroom dance classes. Try to identify these dances.

3. The extended family is very important in Latin American culture. If you read the book *Bruchko*, by Bruce Olson, notice what Olson points out about family life in a Motilone Indian tribe. Share your insights with your family.

OTHER IDEAS/NOTES:

SOUTH AMERICA: CURRENT EVENTS

Use the space below to record the articles you have found or the news that you have heard during your study of South America. Clip out the news articles and glue or paste them to a separate sheet of paper. Insert those pages after this page in your notebook.

Date of Newspaper or Radio/TV Broadcast	Name of Newspaper or News Station	Topic of News Item*
_____	_____	_____
_____	_____	_____
_____	_____	_____
_____	_____	_____
_____	_____	_____
_____	_____	_____
_____	_____	_____

* Examples: National currency, war, leadership, economics, government, environment, social issues, natural disasters (earthquakes, volcano eruptions)

- Notes -

RESOURCES

TEXTBOOKS

GRADE LEVEL	TITLE	AUTHOR/ PUBLISHER
4-6	*Old World History and Geography*	A Beka Book
9-12	*History of the World in Christian Perspective*	A Beka Book
7-12	*World Studies for Christian Schools*	Bob Jones Univ. Press
7-12	*World Geography in Christian Perspective*	A Beka Book

BOOKS OF INTEREST/READERS

4th up	*The Big Wave*	Pearl S. Buck
5th up	*Commodore Perry in the Land of the Shogun*	Blumberg
5th up	*The Mogols*	Nicholson
5th up	*Tales of a Korean Grandmother*	Carpenter
5th up	*Li Lun, Lad of Courage*	Treffinger
5th up	*Ali and the Golden Eagle*	Grover
5th up	*The Samurai's Tale*	Haugaard
6th up	*The Endless Steppe*	Hautzig
6th up	*The Bronze Bow*	Speare
7th up	*The Good Earth*	Buck

MISSIONARIES TO READ ABOUT

Brother Andrew	Mother Teresa	William Carey
J. Hudson Taylor	Amy Carmichael	Hannah Marshman
John and Betty Stam	Jonathan Goforth	Adoniram Judson
Robert Morrison		

OTHER PEOPLE YOU MAY WANT TO READ ABOUT

Genghis Kahn	Kublai Khan	Commodore Perry
Chiang Kai-shek	Marco Polo	Mahatma Ghandi
Mao Tse-tung	Peter the Great	

ASIA: GEOGRAPHY

Use an atlas, encyclopedia, textbooks, and/or library books to find answers to the following questions.

IDENTIFY:

1. the largest continent on earth - *Asia*

2. the highest place on earth - *Mount Everest (located on the Nepal-Tibet border)*

3. the lowest place on earth - *the Dead Sea (located on the border between Israel and Jordan)*

4. the two most populous countries in the world - *China and India*

5. the large desert located in China - *Gobi Desert*

6. the highest mountain in Japan - *Mount Fuji*

7. the basic unit of Japanese currency - *the yen*

8. the two largest cities in China - *Beijing (Peking) and Shanghai*

9. the island which lies off the southern tip of India - *Sri Lanka*

10. the largest sea - *the South China Sea*

11. the warmest ocean - *the Indian Ocean*

12. the largest peninsula - *Arabia*

13. the world's deepest (fresh water) lake - *Lake Baykal (or Baikal), which is located in southern Siberia*

14. the world's greatest archipelago - *Indonesia*

15. the world's largest inland sea - *Caspian Sea*

16. the world's longest wall - *the Great Wall of China*

DEFINE:

1. monsoon - *A wind which originates from the Indian Ocean and southern Asia. From April to October it blows from the southwest and brings heavy rains. The rest of the year it blows from the northeast.*

2. tundra - *a large treeless plain in the arctic regions*

3. alluvial plain - *land which is formed from sediment (gravel, sand, silt) that is left by flooded waters as it recedes back into its banks.*

4. plateau - *a flat land that is higher than the surrounding area; also called a* **tableland** *or* **mesa**

5. valley - *an area of low land which lies between ranges of hills or mountains*

6. archipelago - *a group of islands*

7. delta - *a build-up of soil deposited at the mouth of a river*

GEOGRAPHY QUESTIONS:

1. List the three great fertile river valleys of Asia which were the homes of three important ancient civilizations.

   Tigris-Euphrates Valley   Indus Valley   Yangtze Valley

2. Because Asia is connected to the same landmass as Europe, these two continents together are sometimes called what?

   Eurasia

3. Asia has more mountains than any of the other continents. What benefits and what problems do these mountains cause the people of Asia?

   Benefits: mountain springs are the source of many Asian rivers whose waters are used for irrigation of crops.
   Problems: mountains cause obvious transportation challenges; they also isolate and separate peoples from one another.

5. In which country (or region) can the giant panda be found?

   This white bear-like animal is found only in southwestern China and eastern Tibet.

6. Elephants are found in both Africa and Asia, yet an African elephant is different from an Asian elephant. List some of the differences.

   The African elephant is bigger and has larger ears. The African elephant also has a dip in its back, where the Asian elephant has a hump. The African elephant has a

   smooth, curved forehead; the Asian elephant has two humps on its forehead. The African elephant has four or five toes on its front legs and three on its back legs. The Asian elephant has five toes on the front legs and four on its hind legs. The trunk of the African elephant has two knobs of flesh on its tip. The Asian elephant has one knob of flesh on its trunk. The African elephant has a loose fold of skin on its stomach, which the Asian elephant does not have. The African elephant's tusks are longer than those of the Asian elephant.

7. Japan is made up of how many large islands and how many small islands?

   four large islands and thousands of small islands

8. Give the names of the four major islands.

   Hokkaido   Honshu
   Kyushu   Shikoku.

9. Describe the land form of most of Japan.

   mountainous

   What makes it that way?

   volcanoes

10. What is the capital city of Japan?

    Tokyo

11. What is the average number of earthquakes per year in Japan?

    about 1,500

12. How many volcanoes are located on the Japanese islands?

    150

    How many are active?

    about 60

13. Briefly describe the climate of Japan.

    Japan can get as cold as 20 °below zero (Fahrenheit) in winter, over 80 °in the summer, and rainfall can total 80 inches. There is seasonal change in the weather.

14. By what name is the area in northeastern China often known?

    Manchuria

15. By what name is the area in northwestern China often known?

    Mongolia

16. How did the Yellow River earn the name of "China's Sorrow"?

    Its disastrous floods have claimed so many lives over the centuries.

17. Why is India called a "subcontinent"?

    India is a large peninsula which is separated from the rest of Asia by the Himalayan Mountains.

18. List the three geographic regions that India can be divided into.

    Deccan Plateau　　　*the Himalayan Mountain System*　　　*the Northern Plains*

19. List three important river systems that water the Northern Plains.

    Indus River　　　*Ganges River*　　　*Brahmaputra River*

20. List some of the wildlife that is native to India.

    cobra, elephant, mongoose, rhinoceros, tiger

21. What is India's basic unit of currency?

    the rupee

MAP ACTIVITY. Trace a map of the continent of Asia. Label the following items.

Countries _(Capital Cities)_

____ Afghanistan _(Kabul)_

____ Bangladesh _(Dacca)_

____ Bhutan _(Thimphu)_

____ Burma _(Rangoon)_

____ Cambodia _(Phnom Penh)_

____ China _(Beijing)_

____ India _(New Delhi_ also show: Calcutta, Bombay_)_

____ Yemen Arab Republic _(San'a')_

____ Iran _(Tehran)_

____ Iraq _(Baghdad)_

____ Israel _(Jerusalem)_

____ Japan _(Tokyo)_

____ Jordan _(Amman)_

____ Kuwait

____ Laos _(Vientiane)_

____ Lebanon _(Beirut)_

____ Malaysia _(Kuala Lumpur)_

____ Vietnam _(Hanoi, Ho Chi Minh City)_

____ United Arab Emirates _(Abu Dhabi)_

____ Mongolia _(Ulan Bator)_

____ Nepal _(Kathmandu)_

____ N. Korea _(Pyongyang)_

____ S. Korea _(Seoul)_

____ Oman _(Muscat)_

____ Pakistan _(Islamabad)_

____ Philippines _(Manila)_

____ Qatar _(Doha)_

____ Saudi Arabia _(Riyadh)_

____ Singapore

____ Sri Lanka _(Colombo)_

____ Syria _(Damascus)_

____ Taiwan _(Taipei)_

____ Thailand _(Bangkok)_

____ Turkey _(Ankara)_

____ Maldives _(Male)_

____ Bahrain _(Manama)_

Oceans, Seas, Rivers, Gulfs, Straits

___ East China Sea

___ South China Sea

___ Philippine Sea

___ Bay of Bengal

___ Sea of Okhotsk

___ Bering Strait

___ Indus River

___ Ob River

___ Lake Baykal

___ Pacific Ocean

___ East China Sea

___ Sea of Japan

___ Red Sea

___ Persian Gulf

___ Huang He River

___ Yangtze River

___ Ural River

___ Arabian Sea

___ Yellow Sea

___ Black Sea

___ Caspian Sea

___ Gulf of Aden

___ Ganges River

___ Lena River

___ Dead Sea

Mountains, Deserts, Other Landmarks

___ Himalayan Mountains

___ Siberia

___ Gobi Desert

___ the equator

___ Ural Mountains

___ Mt. Fujiyama

GEOGRAPHY ACTIVITY SUGGESTIONS: *ASIA*

1. Memorize the capitals of several Asian countries.

2. ✑✎ What is the "Ring of Fire"? What does this have to do with the number of earthquakes and volcanoes in Japan? Research and report what you find. (EARTH SCIENCE)

3. ✑✎ Research one animal found in Asia. Write or give a report that tells about this animal's environment--where it lives, what it eats. Also, give the natural enemies of this animal and how it protects itself. How are the young cared for? When are they considered an adult? Add any other interesting information that you find. Draw or cut out a picture of this animal and add to your notebook. (LIFE SCIENCE)

4. ✑✎ Read to find out more about the monsoons of eastern Asia. How do they affect the climate of this area? When is the rainy season? Do monsoons only carry warm, moist air? How much rain will an area get during the monsoon season? Report what you find--either in writing or orally. [EARTH SCIENCE]

5. ✎ Study a product (land-use) map in an atlas. Notice how the map uses a symbol to represent the agricultural products or natural resources produced in a given area. Draw an outline map of Asia and to make your own product map. Use your own symbols and make a key that explains what the symbols represent. Using colored pencils helps to make an attractive and readable map.

6. Study the time zones of the earth. Choose four different cities from this continent. Then calculate what time it is in those cities at the time you are doing this project. [MATH]

7. **[UE/JH]** What happens when an earthquake occurs under water? Look up the word **tsunami** and find out why an ocean earthquake can be as destructive and deadly as one that happens on land. [EARTH SCIENCE]

8. **[UE/JH]** 📄 Most of the subcontinent of India has three seasons. Find out what these three seasons are, then make a chart which describes each season. Share the information with your family.

9. **[UE/JH]** 🖊 Choose four nations from the continent of Asia. Draw and color their flags, state the name of each country's current political leader, list the major exports of each nation, and the nation's unit of currency. Put this information in your notebook.

Other Ideas/Notes:

ASIA: HISTORY

TERMS:

1. dynasty - *a ruling family where the power keeps passing from one family member to another*

2. porcelain - *thin, strong, translucent pottery*

3. calligraphy - *literally, "beautiful writing"*

4. kowtow - *kneeling and touching one's forehead to the ground; done as a token of submission and humility to a superior*

5. opium - *a narcotic derivative of the poppy plant from India; used medicinally, but is also a mind-altering drug*

STUDY QUESTIONS:

1. The Chang (Shang) dynasty was the first of around ten major dynasties in China's history. How long did this family rule?

    about 500 years (1525-1028 BC)   (sources may differ)

2. For what artistic skill were the artisans of the Chang dynasty known?

    bronze work

3. What metals make up "bronze"?

    a mixture of copper, tin, and lead

4. The family that ruled after the Chang family had the longest rule in China's history. Which family was it?

    the Chou family

5. How long was their rule?

    800 years   (1085-221 BC)   (sources may differ)

6. China experienced her "Classical Age" during this family's rule. What makes something "classic"? What does a nation's "Classical Age" offer to later generations?

    A classic is something considered to be the best of its kind. It marks a high point in development. For later generations, it sets a standard against which others of its kind are measured.

7. After the Chou dynasty collapsed, the **Ch'in** family took control. What two lasting "monuments" are left from this dynasty.

    1) The nation's name of "China"   2) the Great Wall of China

8. The next empire was ruled by the **Han** family. List some of the achievements of China during this dynasty.

    a calendar of 365 ¼ days; silk cloth; glazed pottery; paper

9. What was the "Silk Road"?

    the road which linked China with the Roman world for the silk trade

10. During the Medieval Period (beginning AD 500), the Sui, T'ang, and Sung dynasties ruled. During the T'ang and Sung dynasties, China reached her **Golden Age**. What determines a culture's Golden Age?

> *After a civilization's Classical Age, a Golden Age will often follow. Whereas a Classical Age sets the standards and is a model for later generations, the Golden Age is a period of building on the Classical Age. Great cultural achievements mark a Golden Age.*

11. What group of people was the most honored by the time China entered her Golden Age?

> *the scholars*

12. What made a person a "scholar" in China during this time?

> *A scholar was one who thoroughly knew the Confucian <u>Classics</u>. Anyone could be a scholar. It did not depend on family wealth. Studying, taking, and passing many levels of exams were the steps to becoming a scholar.*

13. What types of jobs would these scholars likely have?

> *Only scholars could hold government positions, the most honorable occupation in China. The higher the level of exam passed, the higher the position one could hold in government. This also meant greater wealth and honor.*

14. China had two major periods of trading. The first was during the Han dynasty. The second was during the Yuan dynasty (1279-1368). What items did the other countries want from China?

> *spices, pottery, silk, porcelain vessels, precious gems, primitive cannons, and rockets*

15. What items did China want from the European world?

> *horses, scented woods, precious gems*

16. What religion entered China during this period of extensive trading?

> *Buddhism (from India)*

17. What other two religions still remained strong?

> *Confucianism and Taoism*

18. The Chinese were the ones who learned how to make paper. During the Golden Age, they invented something else which enabled them to have many books and libraries. What was this?

   block printing

19. Name two other inventions that came from the Chinese.

   gunpowder   *magnetic compass*

20. What dynasty ruled from the late 1300s to 1600s?

   the Ming dynasty

21. Which dynasty was in control from 1644 until 1911?

   the Manchu dynasty

22. What was the Ming and Manchu dynasty's attitude toward China's trade with the outside world?

   They did all they could to hamper trade with the western world. The Chinese considered themselves quite superior to the outside world and had no use for any of the western goods.

23. For the little trade that was allowed, which nation controlled most of this trading?

   Great Britain

24. What one product did the British finally find that the Chinese wanted?

   opium

25. After the Opium Wars between China and Great Britain, treaties were signed and trade opened up again between China and the western world. This also opened the door for missionary work. Name two missionaries who spent time in China during this time.

   James Hudson Taylor   *Robert Morrison*   *William Burns*

26. **[HS]** The influx of trade with the western world caused one group of Chinese to rebel and revolt violently. This group of Chinese were called the **Boxers**. Who were they? Who and what did they adamantly oppose?

> *The Boxers were members of a secret group who were officially named the "Society of Righteous and Harmonious Fists". The name of Boxers was a nickname given by the Europeans. The Boxers hated anyone who was a foreigner, especially missionaries. But even their own were not exempt. The Boxers had a deep hatred for the Chinese who had been converted to Christianity. The attacks and killings by this group finally caused European governments to send in troops and make demands that this treatment be stopped and reparations made.*

27. **[HS]** What was one of the results of the Boxer Rebellion?

> *The Manchu dynasty grew weaker and weaker. This rebellion and the ensuing problems with European nations caused the downfall of this last dynasty. A new form of government soon took over.*

28. What was the previous name of the country of Taiwan?

> *Formosa*

    By what other name is Taiwan called?

> *Nationalist China or Republic of China*

29. What land is nicknamed the "Land of the Rising Sun"?

> *Japan*

30. What name did Marco Polo give to the island country of Japan?

> *Cipango*

31. From around 1200 until the middle 1800s, Japan was a feudal aristocratic society. However, instead of kings, knights, and serfs (as in Europe), Japan had a **Mikado, shoguns, daimios, and samurais.** Define each of these roles.

> *Mikado - the emperor*   *shogun - the feudal lord*
> *daimios - local landlords*   *samurai - the warriors/knights*

32. What was Japan's ambition which led to their part in World War II?

> *imperialism (the desire to build a large empire)*

33. What American naval base did Japan attack which led to the United States entering World War II?

> *Pearl Harbor (located in Hawaii)*

34. What Japanese cities were the targets of the first two atomic bombs to be used in warfare?

> *Hiroshima   Nagasaki*

35. After World War II, what happened to the nation of Korea?

> *It was divided into two countries. Russia was given control over North Korea and the United States was given control of South Korea.*

36. What happened in 1950 which caused the Korean War?

> *North Korean Communists invaded South Korea and tried to take control.*

37. What was the result of the Korean War?

> *With the help of the United States, South Korea remained free from Communist control.*

38. **[HS]** When did Hong Kong revert to a Chinese Island? Who previously had a "mandate" on this area?

> *1997   Great Britain*

Suggestions for Further Research on _ASIAN_ History:

1. ✎ Find out more about China's Classical Age. Listed below are several areas influenced by this era. Briefly describe the "classical" way each was handled.

> Chinese Classical Thought
> Chinese Classical Education   _(Note: This information can be found_
> Chinese Classical Rule   _in Bob Jones' World Studies textbook,_
> Chinese Classical Families   _Chapters 5 & 9)_
> Chinese Classical Art

2. Make a time line of the important historical events of this continent. Some points to include would be:

> - Buddha is born
> - Mohammed is born
> - Confucius is born
> - Japan closes its doors to European influence and trade
> - War between China and Great Britain
> - Japan and China at War
> - World War I
> - World War II
> - Vietnam War
> - Chinese Communists conquer mainland China
> - Korean War
> - Civil War in Pakistan; Bangladesh becomes an independent nation

3. Find out more about the opium trade between China and Great Britain. Why were measures finally taken to stop the trade? What affect did this drug have on the Chinese people? How did the British react to the ban on trade? What war was finally fought between these two nations over this drug?

4. During the 1800s when the struggle to have open trade with China was occurring, the Europeans were competing for "spheres of influence". What does this mean? What stopped this from happening?

5. ✎ ✐ The Manchus (Ch'ing Dynasty) were the last ruling dynasty, lasting until 1912. The Boxer Rebellion of 1899 was the "beginning of the end" for the traditional Chinese culture. Research this event and write a report which summarizes the events which followed leading up to the end of the dynasty era.

6. ▤ The continent of Asia contains what is called the "Cradle of Civilization". All the early civilizations have their birth on this continent. Research one or two of these earliest civilizations. List their more notable achievements and report your findings. (Suggested civilizations: Sumerians, Hittites, Phoenicians, Babylonians)

7. **[HS]** Trace the history of China's governments from the collapse of the ancient dynasty system (in 1912) to the present. Include the names of the one/s in power, the type of government, and the effect on the Chinese society.

8. **[UE-HS]** ✎ ✐ Japan shut itself off from the world for 200 years (from the 1600s to the 1800s). Why did they do this? What were the circumstances surrounding its opening up to the outside world again. Give the names of significant people involved. Write a short report on this topic and insert in your notebook.

9. **[HS]** ✎ ✐ During 1997, Hong Kong was a major news topic. Find out why. Try to collect news clippings (by making copies from library sources) and write a summary of Hong Kong's past, present, and predicted political situation. Place this information in your notebook.

10. **[HS]** ✎ ✐ Israel became a nation again in 1948. Trace the path that Israel took in order to re-establish itself as a nation. How has Israel been received by her neighboring countries? List the major wars/conflicts Israel has had with her Arab neighbors. How is this a part of the seemingly constant turmoil in the Middle East today?

Other Ideas/Notes:

ASIA: RELIGION

TERMS

1. theocracy - *a type of government in which God is the ruler*

2. Koran - *the holy book of Islam*

3. reincarnation - *a belief that the soul is reborn into a new body*

4. Muslim - *a follower of the Islam religion*

5. monotheism - *the belief in one God*

6. guru - *a Hindu religious teacher*

7. animism - *a belief that everything in nature has a spirit*

8. Brahman - *the universal spirit of the Hindu religion; it is absolute and impersonal*

STUDY QUESTIONS:

1. Explain the school of thought called **Taoism.**

   Taoists taught that while relationships between people were important, the most important was man's relationship to nature. They said that you should not disturb or control the natural environment, but live with it and enjoy it. This obviously led to the worship of nature.

2. Who is considered the "Father of Modern Missions"? What was his motto?

   William Carey   "Expect great things from God; attempt great things for God."

3. What is the "law of the karma" of the Hindu faith?

   the belief that one's thoughts, actions, and words will decide one's fate in the next life through reincarnation

Suggestions for Further Research on the Religions of *ASIA*

1. ▣ Many churches support missionaries who are working in Asia. Try to make contact with one and ask them about their work, such as: What is your biggest challenge in reaching these people? Are the people receptive to your message? What types of outreach seem to work best? Do you have churches in villages or are they in large cities?

2. ✎ ✐ All the world's major religions have their beginnings in Asia. For each of these major religions (excluding Christianity and Judaism), write a paragraph which summarizes the main beliefs. Include the name of the god worshipped, what is believed about life after death, any rituals that must be performed, and what is upheld as a devout lifestyle. Also tell where (in which countries) each religion is the strongest. The religions to research are:

   BUDDHISM   CONFUCIANISM
   HINDUISM   ISLAM
   SHINTO   TAOISM

3. **[JH/HS]** ✐ Even Christianity and Judaism began in Asia. Which of the above religions has a type of "kinship" with Judaism? In what way? How is this "sibling rivalry" still an issue even today? Write a report that discusses this issue. Use current events to support your answer.

4. ✎ Christianity is the one major world religion that does not have a foothold in most parts of Asia. Why do you think this is so? Mission workers even have a term for the area where their mission efforts have been so challenging. This area is called the **"10-40 Window"**. Try to find out why this term is used.   (Hint: It has something to do with latitude and longitude.)

124

Other Ideas/Notes:

ASIA: CULTURE

TERMS:

1. cuneiform - *the earliest form of writing developed by the Sumerians*

2. ziggurat - *temple-towers (as in the Tower of Babylon)*

3. rickshaw - *(jinrikisha) a two-wheeled carriage pulled by one or more men to carry people*

4. Yiddish - *a language derived from medieval German and spoken by European Jews*

5. suttee - *the Hindu practice of forcing widows to throw themselves upon their husband's funeral pyres*

6. pyre - *a pile of wood used for burning a dead body as a funeral rite*

7. kibbutz - *an Israeli communal farm settlement*

8. sari - *clothing of women in south Asia that consists of a large piece of cloth wrapped around the body*

9. Sanskrit - *the ancient language of India that is held sacred*

10. calico - *a checked or printed cotton material which was first manufactured in Calicut, India (thus named "calico")*

11. kimono - *the traditional long robe (dress) of Japanese women*

12. pagoda – *a far eastern temple built with its roofs curving upward at the division of each of several stories*

STUDY QUESTIONS:

1. What type of painting was the most important during China's Golden Age?

    paintings of landscapes

2. Explain how a Chinese artist (during the Golden Age) would go about painting a landscape picture.

    The artist would look at a scene for a long time while meditating on it. Then he would begin his painting.

3. Why did the Chinese build their houses long and low?

    so that they would blend into the landscape

4. Who invented the rickshaw? What circumstances surrounded this invention?

    Jonathan Goble, a Baptist missionary to Japan, invented it when his wife became very sick and was unable to walk.

5. What is the system called which separates India's people into strict class divisions?

    caste system

6. What is the **Taj Majal**? Where is it and why was it built?

    An ornate white marble building located in the city of Agra in India. It was constructed by a Mogul emperor as a tomb for his favorite wife (1700s).

7. What contributions has India made to world progress?

    In mathematics, they were the first to come up with the number that represented "zero". They developed place value (the modern decimal system), as well as devised the system we know as algebra. They are responsible for creating our modern written numbers, (which are called Arabic numbers). Indians also used chemical principles in the dying of cloth as well as in refining iron ore.

<u>Suggestions for Further Research on the Culture of 𝒜𝒮𝐼𝒜:</u>

1. ☙ ✍ One can't think of Asia without thinking of rice. When most of us picture someone from the Orient we often think of someone standing in a rice paddy. Research how rice is grown. How is it planted? How long does it take to reach maturity? What kind of soil does it need? Report your findings in writing or orally. Add pictures to your report if you can.

2. ☙ ✍ Research the caste system of India. What are the main social divisions?   What are the "rules" of this system? What is an "out-caste"? Include this information as well as any other interesting facts in a report. Share your information with your family and put your findings in your notebook.

3. **[HS]** ☙ ✍ Rural life in Israel differs greatly from that of other Asian nations. Find out what you can about what life would be like on an Israeli kibbutz. Explain how land ownership and labor are shared. Write a short descriptive report for your notebook.

4. **[JH/HS]** ☙ ✍ For a period in India's history, Britain controlled this nation. There were several benefits to India during this time. Research and report what these benefits were.

5. During India's struggle for independence in the early 1900s, two leaders of special note were Mahatma Gandhi and Jawaharlal Nehru. Read about the lives of these two men and summarize the methods they used to help India gain its independence.

128

<u>OTHER IDEAS/NOTES:</u>

ASIA: CURRENT EVENTS

Use the space below to record the articles you have found or the news that you have heard during your study of Asia. Clip out the news articles and glue or paste them to a separate sheet of paper. Insert those pages after this page in your notebook.

Date of Newspaper or Radio/TV Broadcast	Name of Newspaper or News Station	Topic of News Item*
_____	_____	_____
_____	_____	_____
_____	_____	_____
_____	_____	_____
_____	_____	_____
_____	_____	_____
_____	_____	_____

* Examples: National currency, war, leadership, economics, government, environment, social issues, natural disasters (earthquakes, volcano eruptions)

- NOTES -

EUROPE

RESOURCES

TEXTBOOKS

GRADE LEVEL	TITLE	AUTHOR/ PUBLISHER
4-6	*Old World History and Geography*	A Beka Book
9-12	*History of the World in Christian Perspective*	A Beka Book
7-12	*World Geography in Christian Perspective*	A Beka Book
7-12	*World Studies for Christian Schools*	Bob Jones Univ. Press
7-12	*Streams of Civilization*	Christian Liberty Press

BOOKS OF INTEREST/READERS

2nd up	*Pompeii: Buried Alive*	Kunhardt
4th up	*The Door in the Wall*	DeAngeli
4th up	*The Children's Homer*	Colun
5th up	*The Morning Star of the Reformation*	Thompson
5th up	*The Hiding Place*	Ten Boom
5th up	*Shadow of a Bull*	Wojciechowska
5th up	*The Trumpeter of Krakow*	Kelly
6h up	*The Hawk that Dare Not Hunt by Day*	O'Dell
6th up	*Otto of the Silver Hand*	Pyle
6th up	*Adam of the Road*	Vining
6th up	*Snow Treasure*	McSurigan
6th up	*Escape from Warsaw*	Serraillier
6th up	*Shadow of the Bull*	Wojciechowska
9th up	*A Tale of Two Cities*	Charles Dickens
9th up	*Hard Times*	Charles Dickens
9th up	*Julius Caesar*	Shakespeare

MISSIONARIES AND OTHER PEOPLE YOU MAY WANT TO READ ABOUT

Wilberforce	Martin Luther	John Calvin	Wycliffe
Tyndale	Alexander the Great	Napoleon	Hitler
Margaret Thatcher			

(Other musicians, artists, authors, and scientists are listed at the end of the Culture section.)

EUROPE: GEOGRAPHY

Use an atlas, encyclopedia, textbooks, and/or library books to find answers to the following questions.

IDENTIFY:

1. Europe's longest river - *the Volga River*

2. Europe's second longest river - *the Danube River*

3. the European country known as the "land of thousands of lakes" - *Finland*

4. the largest saltwater lake in the world - *Caspian Sea*

5. the major peninsulas that are part of Europe - *Balkan, Iberian, Apennine, Scandinavian, Jutland*

6. the largest mountain system in Europe - *the Alps*

7. the mountain range that divides Spain and France - *the Pyrenees*

8. the mountain range that is the major division between Asia and Europe - *the Urals*

9. the city "set on seven hills" - *Rome*

10. the river which flows through Paris, France - *Seine River*

11. the country known for its colorful **tulip fields** - *the Netherlands*

12. the term which is used when referring to both Europe and Asia as one continent -

    Eurasia

13. the land of "fire and ice" - *Iceland*

14. the home of Hans Christian Andersen - *Denmark*

15. the world's largest island - *Greenland*

16. Europe's highest mountain peak - *Mount Blanc (France)*

17. the location of the Matterhorn - *in the Alps Mountains on the southern border of Switzerland*

DEFINE:

1. fjord - *long, narrow inlets of the sea which cut into a coastline; steep mountain slopes and cliffs usually border the fjord*

2. tundra - *a cold, usually frozen, boggy area in northern Europe (and Asia) along the Arctic coastline. In the summer, the land only thaws on top (about one to two feet deep) causing marshes and swamps to form.*

3. taiga - *cold forest lands in northern regions*

GEOGRAPHY QUESTIONS:

1. What countries are included on the Balkan Peninsula?

    Greece, Albania, Yugoslavia, Bulgaria, and European part of Turkey

2. List three major islands located in the Mediterranean Sea.

    Corsica   Sicily   Sardinia   Cyprus   Crete

3. Name two straits which run from the Mediterranean Sea.

    the Dardanelles   Strait of Gibraltar

4. What is the name of the highest mountain peak in Greece?

    Mt. Olympus

5. What is the name of the active volcano on Sicily's eastern coast?

    Mount Etna

6. Which mountains are called the "backbone of Italy"?

    the Apennines

7. What is the principle river of England?

    the Thames River

8. The Po River is which country's longest river?

    Italy

9. Which European city was once separated by a wall?

    Berlin (Germany)

10. In which city would you find the Cathedral of Notre Dame, the Eiffel Tower, and the Louvre Museum?

    Paris (France)

11. What major city would you find along the Thames River?

    London   (England)

12. In which country would you find the Black Forest?

    Germany

13. In which city would you find streets that were actually water canals?

    Venice (Italy)

14. Where are the sunny beaches called the **Riviera** located?

    in southern France along the shores of the Mediterranean (also in Italy)

15. Name the mountains, the river, and the sea which form Europe's eastern boundary.

    the Ural Mountains, the Ural River, and the Caspian Sea

16. In which area of Europe are **fjords** found?

    the coastline of Norway.

17. What countries are included in the Scandinavian peninsula?

    Norway and Sweden

18. What country is located on the Jutland peninsula?

    Denmark

19. What countries are part of the Iberian peninsula?

    Spain and Portugal

20. Where is the Rock of Gibraltar located?

    Gibraltar is a small peninsula in southern Spain. At its tip is a mountain called the Rock of Gibraltar. This mountain juts into the Strait of Gibraltar, the entrance to the Mediterranean Sea.

21. Where are the White Cliffs of Dover?   Why are they so white?

    *The cliffs are located along the coast of England at the Strait of Dover.
    They are white because the cliffs are made up of chalk.*

22. Italy has two independent states which lie within its borders. What are their names?

    the Republic of San Marino (in north central Italy) and Vatican City (in Rome)

MAP ACTIVITY.   Trace a map of the continent of Europe. Label the following items.

Countries *(Capital Cities)*

___ Albania *(Tiranë)*	___ Andora *(Andorra la Vella)*
___ Armenia *(Yerevan)*	___ Austria *(Vienna)*
___ Azerbaijan *(Baku)*	___ Belarus *(Minsk)*
___ Belgium *(Brussels)*	___ Bosnia and Herzegovina *(Sarajevo)*
___ Bulgaria *(Sofía)*	___ Croatia *(Zagreb)*
___ Czech Republic *(Prague)*	___ Denmark *(Copenhagen)*
___ Estonia *(Tallinn)*	___ Finland *(Helsinki)*
___ France *(Paris)*	___ Georgia *(Tbilisi)*
___ Germany *(Berlin, Bonn)*	___ Gibraltar *(Gibraltar)*
___ Greece *(Athens)*	___ Hungary *(Budapest)*
___ Iceland *(Reykjavik)*	___ Ireland *(Dublin)*
___ Italy *(Rome)*	___ Latvia *(Riga)*
___ Liechtenstein *(Vaduz)*	___ Lithuania *(Vilnius)*
___ Luxembourg *(Luxembourg)*	___ Macedonia *(Skopje)*
___ Malta *(Valletta)*	___ Moldova *(Kishinev)*
___ Monaco *(Monaco)*	___ The Netherlands *(Amsterdam)*
___ Norway *(Oslo)*	___ Poland *(Warsaw)*
___ Portugal *(Lisbon)*	___ Romania *(Bucharest)*
___ Russia *(Moscow)*	___ San Marino *(San Marino)*
___ Slovakia *(Bratislava)*	___ Slovenia *(Ljubljana)*
___ Spain *(Madrid)*	___ Sweden *(Stockholm)*
___ Switzerland *(Bern)*	___ Ukraine *(Kiev)*

United Kingdom: ___ England *(London)*   ___ Wales *(Cardiff)*
                ___ N. Ireland *(Belfast)*   ___ Scotland *(Edinburgh)*

___ Yugoslavia *(Belgrade)*	___ Balearic Island
___ Corsica	___ Crete
___ Sardinia	___ Sicily

Oceans, Seas, Rivers, Gulfs, Straits

___ Atlantic Ocean	___ Mediterranean Sea	___ Norwegian Sea
___ Black Sea	___ Aegean Sea	___ Bay of Biscay
___ North Sea	___ Adriatic Sea	___ Persian Gulf
___ Caspian Sea	___ Black Sea	___ Baltic Sea
___ Irish Sea	___ Ionian Sea	___ Volga River
___ Danube River	___ Rhine River	___ Oder River
___ Seine River	___ Po River	___ Rhône River
___ Thames River	___ Dnieper River	___ Elbe River
___ English Channel	___ Strait of Gibraltar	___ the Dardanelles

Mountains

___ Alps Mountains	___ Pyrenees Mountains	___ Apennines Mountains
___ Ural Mountains	___ Mt. Vesuvius	___ Mt. Etna
___ Caucasus Mountains		

GEOGRAPHY ACTIVITY SUGGESTIONS: EUROPE

1. Memorize the capitals of several European countries.

2. **[UE/JH]** 📖 ✍ Research one animal found in Europe. Write or give a report that tells about this animal's environment--where it lives, what it eats. Also, give the natural enemies of this animal and how it protects itself. How are the young cared for? When are they considered an adult? Add any other interesting information you find out. Draw or cut out a picture of this animal and add to your notebook. (LIFE SCIENCE)

3. Study a product (land-use) map in an atlas. Notice how the map uses a symbol to represent the agricultural products or natural resources produced in a given area. Use the provided outline map of Europe and make your own product map. ✏ Use your own symbols and make a key that explains what the symbols represent. Using colored pencils helps to make an attractive and readable map.

4. Study the time zones of the earth. Choose two different cities from this continent. Then calculate what time it is in those cities at the time you are doing this project. [MATH]

5. 📖 ✍ Europe contains some excellent agricultural land. Choose a country and find out what agricultural products are grown and exported. Write a brief report of your findings to include in your notebook. (Suggested countries: FRANCE, ITALY, SPAIN)

6. Compare the latitude of Europe and North America. Are their climates similar or different. If different, how are they different and what contributes to this difference? Orally share the information with the rest of your family.

Other Ideas/Notes:

EUROPE: HISTORY

TERMS:

1. helots - *slaves (ancient Greece)*

2. pedagogue - *a well-educated slave who looked after a Greek boy, making sure he did his school work and behaved himself*

3. polis - *a city-state in ancient Greece*

4. barbarians - *rough, uneducated people*

5. dictator - *a person who has absolute rule over a country*

6. patrician - *a person from a wealthy and distinguished family in the Roman Republic*

7. plebeian - *a common person (farmer, peasant) of the Roman Republic.*

8. gladiator - *an armed Roman fighter who fought and killed an unarmed man as a spectator sport*

9. feudalism - *the medieval way of life involving castles, kings, knights, lords, etc.*

10. Renaissance - *a revival of learning based on the philosophy of the ancient Greeks*

11. Reformation - *a revival of learning and study of the Scripture leading to a desired "reforming" of the Roman Catholic Church*

STUDY QUESTIONS:

1.   What were the two most influential early civilizations on the European continent?

     the ancient Greek and Roman civilizations

2.   During what time period did the Greeks attain the high point of their civilization?

     during the 400s and 300s BC

3.   What were the two most famous city-states of ancient Greece?

     Athens and Sparta

4.   What great leader from Macedonia (a kingdom north of Greece) conquered Greece in the 300s BC and became the ruler of Europe's first great empire?

     Alexander the Great

5.   During what time period did the Roman civilization extend?

     from the 200s BC until the AD 400s

6.   The Roman Empire enjoyed approximately 200 years of peace. What is the term for this period of the Early Roman civilization?

     Pax Romana

7.   What great religion began during the height of the Roman Civilization in Palestine (an Asian country which was part of the Roman Empire)?

     Christianity

8.   There were many reasons for the fall of the Roman Empire, but the physical reason was the invasion by several barbarian tribes from the north. What were the names of some of these tribes?

     Angles, Jutes, and Saxons (invaded Roman-held Great Britain)
     Vandals (conquered the area of Spain)
     Visigoths (invaded the Italian peninsula and sacked Rome)
     Franks (conquered most of the area of France)

9. **[HS]** As mentioned in question #8, the Roman Empire fell because of outside attacks. However, history records that Rome really "fell from within". Briefly state what is meant by that statement.

> *During the time of the Roman Republic, there was a sense of strong family unity, and children were trained in the Roman ideals consisting of a sense of duty, seriousness of purpose, and a sense of personal worth ("pietas", "gravitas", "dignitas"). As the empire grew, the family unit disintegrated. Along with this disintegration came the loss of the Roman ideals.*

10. As the Roman Empire began falling apart, it split into two separate sections. What were these two areas called? What was the capital city for each?

> *Western Roman Empire (capital city: Rome)*
> *East Roman, or Byzantine, Empire (capital city: Constantinople)*

11. What is the time period called which begins with the fall of the Roman Empire and ends with the Reformation?   (approximately AD 500 - AD 1500)

> *The Middle Ages (or the Dark Ages)*

12. What sickness caused the death of almost a fourth of Europe's population during the 1300s?

> *the bubonic plague (or Black Death)*

13. As the feudal system of Europe declined, the individual nations began to take shape. What were the earliest nations to assume some form of power?

> *England, France, Portugal, Spain*

14. The Great Renaissance period took place at the end of the Middle Ages. How long did this period last?

> *approximately 300 years (early 1300s to the 1500s)*

15. In which country did the Renaissance begin?

> *Italy*

16. After what ancient cultures did the people of the Renaissance try to model themselves after?

> *the cultures of the ancient Greek and Roman civilizations*

17. What invention of the 1440s helped spread the ideas of the Renaissance throughout Europe?

    Johannes Gutenberg's movable type printing press

18. What was the first book printed on the new printing press?

    the Bible

Special Note:

**The Renaissance and Reformation deserve an in-depth study.
This study guide is not designed for that purpose.
If you choose to go into that study at this time, there are
many resources and biographies available.**

**Another topic of European/Asian history which
deserves study is the recent dividing up of
the former USSR. This can also be studied
in context with Communism and/or government.**

Suggestions for Further Research on EUROPEAN History:

1. **[JH/HS]** 📄 The following individuals lived during the classical Greek era. List each person's name on another sheet of paper; then locate information about each individual in an encyclopedia or world history text. Beside each name, give a brief description of his contribution to history.

Socrates	Archimedes	Pythagoras
Plato	Euclid	Aristarchus
Aristotle	Herodotus	Hippocrates
Homer		

2. Make a time line of the important historical events of this continent. Some points to include would be:

    - **Peak of Classical Greek civilization**
    - **Peak of the Roman empire**
    - **End of Roman Republic/Beginning of Roman Empire**
    - **Beginning of the Middle Ages**
    - **the Crusades**
    - **the Black Death** (killing one-fourth of Europe's population)
    - **the Renaissance** (begins in Italy)
    - **Christopher Columbus-- first European to reach New World**
    - **the Reformation**
    - **the French Revolution**
    - **the Industrial Revolution**
    - **World War I**
    - **the Russian Revolution**
    - **World War II**

3. 📄 List some of the contributions of the Greek and Roman civilizations to western culture. Include areas such as law, art, mathematics, literature, architecture, and drama.

4. **[JH]** 📖 ✏ Read about the Roman Empire in a history text or other reference book. Find out the names of the Roman dictators and make a list. Then next to each name, briefly explain why he was considered a "good" ruler or a "bad" ruler.

5. **[HS]** 📚 ✎ The principles of Roman law are the basis for many western European nations. The **Justinian Code** contains these principles. Research the heritage that Rome has given to the field of law. Compare and contrast what you learn with the American form of law as well as the civil law of other nations.

6. **[HS]** 📄 What Latin words are still used today in the field of law and government? Make a list to add to your notebook.

7. **[UE/JH]** 📚 ✎ Read and find out as much as you can about the feudal system. What was life like in a castle? What were the jobs of the **serf** (peasant), the **lord**, the **knight**, and the **king**? Write a short report that includes the information you found.

8. **[UE/JH]** 🔧 Build a Lego® Block castle. Read first to find out what a typical castle looked like. How was it laid out? What was the "keep". When you finish, show your work to your family and explain all the sections of your castle. (Suggestion: Take a picture of your castle to put it in your notebook!)

9. **[UE/JH]** ✏ Draw a floor diagram of the layout of a typical castle. Attach a report that lists the various parts of the castle and the purpose of each area. Share your diagram with the rest of your family and then place in your notebook.

10. **[UE/JH]** 📚 Read about the life of a medieval knight. What type of training did he have to go through to become a knight? What was his main job as part of a feudal community? Tell what you learn either in writing or orally.

11. **[JH/HS]** 📚 ✎ The **Magna Carta** is one of the most important documents in history. What is this document? When was it written? By whom and for whom? Why was it written? Where was it signed? What were the long-term results of this document? Research this topic and write a report to include in your notebook.

12. **[JH/HS]** ✍ The invention of the printing press has been said to be the "greatest invention of all history". Write an essay supporting this statement.   [COMPOSITION]

13. **[UE/JH]** 📚 Read about the young girl of French history, Joan of Arc. Who was she? What did she do? What were the results of her actions? Tell the rest of your family what you learned about her.

14. **[JH/HS]** 📚 ✍ Find out what you can about the **Reconquista** that took place in Spain in the 1000s. Write a paragraph summary of this event in Europe's history to put in your notebook.

15. **[JH/HS]** 📚 ✍ King Ferdinand and Queen Isabella are best remembered for their support of Christopher Columbus' voyage to the New World. However, they are also less favorably remembered in history as the initiators of the **Spanish Inquisition.** Research this event and write a short paper to add to your notebook.

16. 📚 ✍ Read about the history of Scotland and Wales and their fight for freedom. Read particularly about Sir William Wallace and Robert the Bruce. Give a summary of your research to your family.

17. **[HS]** 📚 The French Revolution is one of the bloodiest revolutions in history. After gathering the historical background of the situation, read **A Tale of Two Cities** by Charles Dickens. (There is also a video available that could be watched by <u>older</u> children.)   (LITERATURE)

18. **[HS]** There has been a big political division as well as a cultural difference between Eastern Europe and Western Europe. What has contributed to this difference? Teach this information to your younger siblings.

Other Ideas/Notes:

EUROPE: RELIGION

DEFINE:

1. martyr - *one who willingly dies for his belief rather than denying it*

2. catacomb - *underground passages and rooms used as cemeteries*

3. monastery - *a home for those who dedicated their life to the Roman Catholic Church*

4. monk - *one who lived in a monastery*

5. pilgrimage - *a trip taken for a religious purpose*

6. indulgence - *a paper which said a person's sins had been forgiven by the pope*

STUDY QUESTIONS:

1. Jesus Christ lived during the time of the great Roman Empire. It wasn't very long after his death, however, when it became a crime to be a "Christian". Who was the Roman emperor who declared it a crime to be a Christian?

    Nero (fifth emperor of the Roman Empire, AD 54-68)

2. How long did the persecution of Christians go on in the Roman Empire?

    approximately 300 years

3. Which Roman emperor brought relief to the severe treatment Christians endured during this time?

    Constantine

4. During the Middle Ages, the Muslims had conquered the Middle East (the birthplace of Jesus). This angered the European Christians because they could no longer freely travel to the Holy Lands. What did they do to try to free Palestine from Muslim control?

    The Pope called for the people to take up arms and fight against the Muslims. A series of battles called "Crusades" took place over a period of several years.

5. Who was John Wycliffe? What did he do? What is he often called?

    John Wycliffe is called the "Morning Star of the Reformation". In the 1300s (200 years before the Reformation), he spoke out against the Catholic Church's position that only priests could read the Bible. Believing that everyone had a right to read the Bible for themselves, he became the first man to translate the entire Bible into the English language.

6. **[HS]** What is the Protestant Reformation?

    [UE/JH] Who is responsible for beginning the Protestant Reformation movement?

    The Protestant Reformation began when Martin Luther, a monk, made a list of 95 reasons why certain activities of the Roman Catholic Church were wrong according to the Bible. He nailed this list up on a door of a church in Wittenburg, Germany, on October 31, 1517. This began the movement which caused a new group to split from the Catholic Church. His "protest" and desire to "reform" the church caused Luther to be brought to trial and expelled from the church.

Suggestions for Further Research on the Religion of EUROPE

1. **[JH/HS]** 📚 ✍ Read about the Crusades of the Middle Ages. Who called the people to action? Why were they fought? What were the names of the major crusades? What happened during the Children's Crusade? What was the result of the people's efforts? Was Jerusalem freed? What kinds of changes did the Crusades bring about to the European way of life? Write a report to include in your notebook.

2. **[JH/HS]** 📚 ✍ Europe has many Christian heroes in its history. Look up the following people and explain their contribution to the Christian faith. Some of them had many followers. Tell what the group believed. Some were martyred. Explain why they were killed and how they were killed.

Peter of Bruis (Petrobruscans)	**Peter Waldo** (Waldensians)
John Wycliffe (Lollards)	**John Huss** (Hussites)
Thomas à Kempis	**Johann Wessel**
Erasmus	

3. **[HS]** 📚 ✍ As the Protestant Reformation spread throughout Europe, many denominations formed from various teachings and beliefs. Research to find at least three of these original groups. Who was their leader? What did he teach? What modern churches have their roots in this early church? Give your findings in a report for your notebook.

Other Ideas/Notes:

EUROPE: CULTURE

As with any of the continents studied so far, the culture will vary with any given area. Europe is no different. Even though it is one of the smallest continents, it has a large number of separate and independent nations with different languages, different currencies, and different types of governments, etc. Another aspect to think about when studying the culture of this continent is the fact that we, as Americans, have received a lot of our nation's own culture, our way of life, from our European forefathers. Although the United States is indeed a type of "melting pot", it is still from Europe that we have received the largest portion of who we are as Americans.

So, for this section of study, this study guide will offer you a "quick quiz" so that you can check your own knowledge and understanding of some of the things that are quite "European". After taking the "quiz", go to your local library (preferably the children's section!) and browse through as many books on as many European countries as your study schedule will allow.

Here's the "QUIZ": Write down the European country that comes to mind when you read the following word or phrase:

1. OPERA - *Italy*

2. PASTRIES - *France; Denmark*

3. SAUERKRAUT - *Germany*

4. HAUTE CUISINE - *France*

5. WINDMILLS - *the Netherlands*

6. RHAPSODIES - *Hungary*

7. BAGPIPES - *Scotland*

8. A LEANING TOWER - *Italy*

9. GYPSIES - *Romania*

10. BULL FIGHTS - *Spain*

11. TULIPS - *the Netherlands*

12. FASHION - *France*

13. PIZZA, SPAGHETTI - *Italy*

14. "THE SOUND OF MUSIC" - *Austria*

15. OKTOBERFEST - *Germany*

16. EIFFEL TOWER - *France*

17. BIG BEN - *England*

18. CHALETS - *Switzerland*

19. "EL CID" - *Spain*

20. RUGBY - *England*

21. WOODEN SHOES - *the Netherlands*

22. FLAMENCO DANCERS - *Spain*

23. NOTRE DAME - *France*

24. ZEUS - *Greece*

25. ST. PATRICK'S DAY - *Ireland*

26. KILTS - *Scotland*

27. BUCKINGHAM PALACE - *England*

28. COLISEUM - *Italy*

Suggestions for Further Research on the Culture of EUROPE:

1. **[UE]** The setting for many of the Grimm fairy tales is the Black Forest of Germany. Who is "Grimm" of these fairly tales? What are the names of some of the stories? 📖 Read one of these fairly tales and then design a book cover for the story. Be sure to add the title of the story on your book cover. Add this drawing to your notebook.

2. Many of the world's greatest scientists, musicians, and artists have come from the continent of Europe. Several are listed below. Choose one of the following activities to do:

   📖 Read a biography. (Why not try one biography from each group!). Then write a short summary of this person's life to include in your notebook. Share something about this person's life with the rest of your family.

   📖 Choose three or more from each group. Look up each person to find his most important contribution/s to history. Make a list of what you find to add to your notebook.

   scientists: Johann Kepler
   Albert Einstein (later became an American citizen)
   Louis Pasteur
   Pierre and Marie Curie
   Galileo Galilei
   Michael Faraday
   Lord Kelvin

   musicians: Johann Sebastian Bach
   George Frederick Handel
   Ludwig van Beethoven
   Rimsky-Korsakov
   Tchaikovsky

   artists: Rembrandt   Reubens
   Van Gogh   Michelangelo
   Leonardo da Vinci   Raphael
   Verdi   Puccini
   El Greco   Albrecht Dürer
   Jan Van Eyck   Lorenzo Ghiberti

3. Several well-known authors also come from Europe. Look up the following people in an encyclopedia and list one or two of their most prominent works.

Hans Christian Andersen	Miguel de Cervantes
William Shakespeare	Anton Chekhov
Robert Browning	Leo Tolstoy
Charles Dickens	Alexander Solzhenitsyen
Rudyard Kipling	John Bunyan
Robert Louis Stevenson	John Milton
Daniel Defoe	Johann Wyss
Mary Mapes Dodge	Johanna Spyri

4. [UE/JH] Choose at least four countries from Europe and draw and color the flags of those countries. Use a separate sheet of paper for each country. Use the bottom half of the paper to list the nation's unit of currency, the current political leader, the type of government, and the capital city.

5. One can't think of Italy without thinking of pizza and spaghetti. Are they truly Italian dishes? Are they popular all over the country or are they regional dishes? Research the cuisine of Italy. After doing a thorough research, why not volunteer to prepare a meal for your family--complete with a report on what you've learned! (P. S. Be sure to serve some *antipasto*!)

6. Watch, or listen to, an Italian opera. Some preliminary study would probably make the listening more enjoyable and aid in one's understanding. What is the history of opera? Who have been some of the opera greats (both past and present). Use the information you find to give a presentation to your family (with a sampling of the music included).

7. Occasionally on the news you may hear of someone having money in a Swiss bank account. Why are people interested in placing their money in a bank in Switzerland?

156

<u>OTHER IDEAS/NOTES:</u>

EUROPE: CURRENT EVENTS

Use the space below to record the articles you have found or the news that you have heard during your study of Europe. Clip out the news articles and glue or paste them to a separate sheet of paper. Insert those pages after this page in your notebook.

Date of Newspaper or Radio/TV Broadcast	Name of Newspaper or News Station	Topic of News Item*
_____	_____	_____
_____	_____	_____
_____	_____	_____
_____	_____	_____
_____	_____	_____
_____	_____	_____
_____	_____	_____

* Examples: National currency, war, leadership, economics, government, environment, social issues, natural disasters (earthquakes, volcano eruptions)

~NOTES~

NORTH AMERICA

RESOURCES

TEXTBOOKS

GRADE LEVEL	TITLE	AUTHOR/ PUBLISHER
4-6	*New World History and Geography*	A Beka Book
4-6	*Heritage Studies, grade 5*	Bob Jones Univ. Press
4-9	*World History Series: Exploration & Discovery*	Usborne
4-9	*A History of US Book One: The First Americans*	Joy Hakim
7-12	*World Geography in Christian Perspective*	A Beka Book

READERS

3-up	*Leif the Lucky*	D'Aulaire
3-up	*Dakota Dugout*	Ann Turner
3-up	*The Light and the Glory for Children*	Peter Marshall
3-up	*Calico Captive*	Elizabeth Speare
4-up	*Tikta' Liktak*	Houston
5-up	*Streams to the River, River to the Sea*	Scott O'Dell
6-up	*Water Sky*	George
6-up	*The Light and the Glory*	Peter Marshall
7-up	*The Last of the Mohicans*	James F. Cooper

PEOPLE YOU MAY WANT TO READ ABOUT

Leif Ericson   Christopher Columbus   Sir Wilfred Grenfell

⇨ **Please Note:** Although Mexico and Central America are technically part of the North American continent, the study of this area is included with South America because of their cultural similarities.

North America: GEOGRAPHY

Use an atlas, encyclopedia, textbooks, and/or library books to find answers to the following questions.

IDENTIFY:

1. the highest mountain in North America - *Mount McKinley (Alaska)*

2. the lowest place in North America - *Death Valley*

3. the world's largest fresh water lake - *Lake Superior*

4. the world's largest island - *Greenland*

5. the world's largest prairie - *the North American Plains which stretch from the Mississippi River to the Rocky Mountains and from the Hudson Bay to the Gulf of Mexico*

6. the only Great Lake located totally within the borders of the US - *Lake Michigan*

7. the largest national park in the US - *Denali National Park and Preserve (In Alaska) Yellowstone National Park is the largest in the contiguous United States.*

8. the largest canyon in the world - *the Grand Canyon*

9. the deepest canyon in the US - *Hells Canyon (on the border between Washington and Idaho)*

10. the deepest lake in the US - *Crater Lake (in southwestern Oregon)*

11. the highest peak in the continental US - *Mount Whitney (in California)*

12. North America's highest waterfalls - *Yosemite Falls (in Yosemite National Park)*

13. a famous geyser - *Old Faithful (in Yellowstone National Park)*

14. the first English colony in North America - *Roanoke (However, it didn't last!)*

15. the first permanent colony in North America - *Jamestown (Virginia)*

DEFINE:

1. canal - *a narrow man-made channel of water which joins other bodies of water.*

2. iceberg - *a large broken piece of glacier*

3. glacier - *a large mass of ice and snow*

4. ice shelf - *a large floating sheet of ice*

5. prairie - *a large area located within the temperate zone and is covered by tall grasses; can be flat or hilly*

6. tumbleweed - *round, dried-up plants which are blown across the prairie*

7. tributary - *a smaller river that flows into a major river*

8. hot spring - *a natural spring which has a water temperature above 98°F*

9. geyser - *columns of hot spring water which spout up out of the earth into the air*

GEOGRAPHY QUESTIONS:

1. Where is North America's continental divide located?

    the Rocky Mountains

2. List three tributaries to the Mississippi River.

    Missouri River   Arkansas River   Ohio River
    Tennessee River   Red River

3. List three deserts located in North America.

    Great Basin Desert, Mojave Desert, Sonoran Desert,
    *   Chihuahuan Desert, Colorado Plateau, Painted Desert*

4. Why are almost all the lakes in the Great Basin Desert region salty?

    These lakes have no outlets which would carry the salts away to the sea.

5. Where is the world's tallest tree located? What kind of tree is it?

    in California   California redwood

6. What is the name of another very large tree that grows in the Sierra Nevada Range?

    the giant sequoia

7. What are some of Canada's natural resources?

    forests (harvested pulpwood used to make newsprint)
    fertile soil (one of world's largest producers of wheat)
    fishing   mining

8. What are some of the natural resources of the United States?

    agriculture   natural gas   coal   petroleum
    iron ore   silver   copper

9. Name two animals which can only be found in North America.

    coyotes pronghorns

10. For what is the "General Sherman Tree" of Sequoia National Park famous?

   It is supposed to be the world's largest tree in volume of wood.

11. Give the name of the peninsula which extends south of the state of California.

   Baja (or Lower) California

12. Where and what is the Piedmont Plateau?

   "Piedmont" means "at the foot of the mountains". The Piedmont Plateau of North America slopes from the eastern edge of the Appalachian Mountains to the Atlantic coastal area.

13. What famous ship sank in the North Atlantic Ocean after striking an iceberg?

   The Titanic

MAP ACTIVITY. Trace a map of the continent of North America. Label the following items.

Major Points of Geographic Interest *(Capital Cities)*

___ Canada *(Ottawa)*   ___ Nova Scotia (*Halifax*)   ___ Quebec *(Quebec)*
___ Alberta *(Edmonton)*   ___ Ontario *(Toronto)*   ___ Manitoba *(Winnipeg)*
___ Yukon *(Whitehorse)*   ___ Saskatchewan (*Regina*)
___ Newfoundland *(St. John's)* ___ British Columbia *(Victoria)*
___ New Brunswick *(Fredericton)*
___ Northwest Territories *(Yellowknife)*   ___ United States *(Washington, D.C.)*
___ Prince Edward Island *(Charlottetown)*   ___ Alaska *(Juneau)*

Key Cities

___ Chicago   ___ New York   ___ San Francisco   ___ Los Angeles
___ Denver   ___ Miami   ___ Seattle   ___ Boston
___ New Orleans   ___ Indianapolis   ___ Dallas   ___ Atlanta
___ Phoenix   ___ Detroit   ___ Anchorage   ___ Montreal

Islands

___ Baffin Island   ___ Victoria Island   ___ Vancouver Island
___ Aleutian Islands   ___ Greenland [**belongs to Denmark, but in western hemisphere)**

Oceans, Seas, Rivers, Gulfs, Straits

___ Atlantic Ocean   ___ Pacific Ocean   ___ Hudson Bay

___ James Bay   ___ Hudson Strait   ___ Davis Strait

___ Baffin Bay   ___ Beaufort Sea   ___ Bay of Fundy

___ Foxe Basin   ___ Great Bear Lake   ___ Great Slave Lake

___ Lake Winnipeg   ___ Gulf of St. Lawrence   ___ St. Lawrence River

___ Sault Ste. Marie Canal ___ Lake Superior   ___ Lake Michigan

___ Lake Huron   ___ Lake Erie   ___ Lake Ontario

___ Great Salt Lake   ___ Mississippi River   ___ Colorado River

___ Ohio River   ___ Rio Grande River   ___ Gulf of Mexico

___ Bering Strait   ___ Niagara Falls

Mountains, Deserts, and other features

___ Rocky Mountains   ___ Appalachian Mountains   ___ Cascade Mountains

___ Sierra Nevada Mtns. ___ Adirondack Mtns.   ___ Grand Canyon

___ Ozark Mtns.   ___ Death Valley

GEOGRAPHY ACTIVITY SUGGESTIONS: North America

1. Memorize the capitals of the Canadian provinces.

2. Choose three of the "key cities" listed on the "Map Activity" page. Determine the latitude and longitude of each city. Record this information and place in your notebook.

3. If you have not done so, memorize the capitals of the 50 United States.

Other Ideas/Notes:

NORTH AMERICA: HISTORY

TERMS:

1. portage - *carrying a canoe overland from one river to another (a French term)*

2. galleon - *a big, three-masted Spanish ship*

3. privateer - *a privateer is a pirate ship which "pirated" with the backing their nation's leader*

4. colonies - *settlements of people in a land away from their homeland, but who are still ruled by their mother country*

5. mercantilism - *the belief that a colony exists for the benefit of its mother country*

6. sea dogs - *pirates*

STUDY QUESTIONS:

1. Why are the native Americans called "Indians"?

    *When Christopher Columbus first landed in the New
        World, he actually thought that he had found the
        water route to the East Indies. Therefore, he
        thought the inhabitants of the land were "Indians".*

2. List several native American Indian tribes of the North American continent.

    *Apache, Hopi, Iroquois, Sioux, Cree, Ottawa, Cherokee, Chickasaw,
        Hopewell, Creek, Natchez, Mohawk, Shawnee, Choctaw, Seminole,
        Wampanoags, Delaware, Powhatan, Pueblo, Zuni, Navajo, etc.*

3. Who were probably the first people to arrive on the North American continent?

    the Vikings

4. Approximately when did these people arrive?

    AD 1000

5. Who were the Vikings?

    Seafaring men from the North: Norway, Sweden, Denmark, Iceland, Greenland

6. Who was the first man from <u>any</u> country (besides the Vikings) to land on the
    North American continent?

    John Cabot (of England)

7. Who was trying to find the **Fountain of Youth**?

    Ponce de León

8. Who discovered the Grand Canyon?

    Francisco de Coronado

9. What was he actually searching for when the Grand Canyon was found?

    the Seven Cities of Cibola (a supposed city made of gold and silver)

10. List the name of the ships which carried the following groups to the New World:

> Christopher Columbus and his crew - *the Niña, the Pinta, and the Santa Maria*

> the Pilgrims - *the Mayflower*

> the Jamestown settlers - *the Susan Constant, the Godspeed, and the Discovery*

11. What two groups of people were aboard the *Mayflower*?

> *the Strangers (who were seeking adventure) and the Separatists (those who came in search of religious freedom*

12. Who was the second Governor of Plymouth and what book did he write?

> *William Bradford; he wrote the book, Of Plymouth Plantation*

13. What document was sent by the American colonists to King George of England which listed the grievances they held against his leadership and which said they now considered themselves an independent country?

> *the Declaration of Independence*

14. On what day was the above document signed by representatives from the 13 colonies?

> *July 4, 1776*

15. How long had the United States been an independent nation when it found itself internally divided and at war with itself?

> *about 80 years*

<u>Suggestions for Further Research on NORTH AMERICAN History:</u>

1. ✎ Listed below are three Indian chiefs who were involved in different battles. Research to find the conflict behind each battle as well as who the leader was for the other side. Write out what you find for a report or share the information orally with your family.

    Cochise   **Geronimo**   **Sitting Bull**

2. Make a time line of the important historical events of this continent. Some points to include would be:

    - discovery of the New World by European explorers
    - Canada becomes an independent nation
    - United States becomes an independent nation
    - the American Civil War
    - World War I
    - World War II

3. Find which states in the US have Indian names. If you can, find the meanings of those names as well. Make a list to include in your notebook. You may want to include names of rivers and other landmarks as well.

4. ✎ Canada has often had troubles throughout its history with unity among its people. Even in recent history, some groups in the province of Quebec were campaigning to have Quebec recognized as an independent country separate from the rest of Canada. Look for news articles about the movement and read them in light of Canada's British and French heritage. How did the trouble begin? How has it developed? What do you think is a workable solution? Use this topic to write an essay to include in your notebook.

5. What is the relationship between Canada and the United States? If you were to travel to Canada, could you do so like you were traveling state to state in the United States? Or is there something else involved?

6.   📄 During the Age of Exploration, the land and waterways of North America were explored, charted, and named by many European explorers. Make a chart that lists the explorer, the country each was from, and what he charted, explored, or named. Insert the chart in your notebook. The following explorers should be included:

John Cabot   **Juan Rodrigues Cabrillo**
Amerigo Vespucci   **Vasco de Balboa**
Juan Ponce de León   **Hernando Cortés**
Ferdinand Magellan   **Jacques Cartier**
Hernando de Soto   **Francisco Coronado**
Vasco da Gama   **Sir Walter Raleigh**
Francis Drake   **John White**
Champlain   **Louis Joliet**
Jacques Marquette

7.   A study of the Mound Builder Indians can easily be done in the Midwest. Near Evansville, Indiana, is an excellent museum of excavations and reconstruction of how these Indians lived. The area is called Angel Mounds State Historic Site. In Ohio on Route 73 is Serpent Mound located just northwest of Locust Grove. Also in Ohio is Mound City Group National Monument located north of Chillicothe on Route 104. Cahokia Mounds is just off Route 55 near Collinsville, Illinois.

8.   List all the wars that the United States has been involved in during its 200 years of existence. Briefly tell who each war was fought with and   over what issue.

9.   Memorize all the Presidents of the United States in order of office.

10. Compare and contrast the two types of governments of Canada and the United States.

<u>Other Ideas/Notes:</u>

NORTH AMERICA: RELIGION

DEFINE:

1. Protestant - *one who "protests" or disagrees with the teachings of the Roman Catholic Church*

STUDY QUESTIONS:

1. What are the two largest religious groups in Canada?

   Catholics and Protestants

2. How was Christianity introduced to Canada?

   through the early French traders who brought Catholicism with them

3. Who was the first foreign missionary <u>from</u> America?

   Adoniram Judson

4. Name the prominent denomination of the circuit-riding preachers of the 1800s in the United States.

   Methodists

Suggestions for Further Research on the Religion of NORTH AMERICA

1. Research some of the teachings of the Roman Catholic Church and find out what was being "protested" by the leaders of the Protestant Reformation.

2. Why did the Separatists want to "separate" from the Church of England? Find out the disagreements they had with the English church.

3. 📖 ✍ Among the European settlers were some who worked as missionaries among the various Native American tribes. Listed below are a few of them. Read to find out something about at least two of them. Write a brief summary of their work and include any special contributions or accomplishments.

     John Eliot   **Roger Williams**   **David Brainerd**
     John Wesley   **Charles Wesley**

4. 📖 ✍ What are the top ten Protestant churches in the United States? Choose two of them (which are different from your own church) to research. Compare and contrast their teachings with your church's teaching.

Other Ideas/Notes:

NORTH AMERICA: CULTURE

DEFINE:

1. maize - *another name for corn*

2. mukluks - *boots made from the skin of seals (worn by Eskimos)*

3. syllabary - *a type of alphabet with the symbols representing syllables rather than individual letters*

4. adobe - *sun-dried bricks*

5. wampum - *a type of necklace or belt of purple and white beads, considered to be of value, and used as a type of money especially with European settlers and traders*

6. potlatch - *an Indian feast*

STUDY QUESTIONS:

1. What does the word "Eskimo" literally mean?

    "eaters of raw meat"

2. What do the Eskimos call themselves?

    Inuits

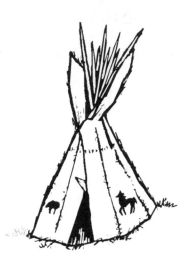

3. Not all Indians lived in teepees. Name some other
    types of Indian homes.

    *wigwams, long houses, pueblos (rooms carved
    into solid rock), hogans, wickiups*

4. Which American Indian developed a syllabary for his tribe?
    Why did he do this?

    *Sequoya was a Cherokee and thought that if his people could read and
    write they could remain free.*

5. What other language besides English is spoken in Canada? In what area?

    French   in Quebec

Suggestions for Further Research on the Culture of North America

1.   Listed below are several Native Americans who are remembered for some type of contribution or action. Find why they are remembered in history. List the ones you have researched and include their accomplishment/s. Add to your notebook after sharing with your family.

   Joseph Brant   **Will Rogers**
   Sequoya   **Massasoit**
   Sacagawea   **Squanto**

2.   The life of the many Indian tribes varied not only from region to region, but also from tribe to tribe. Choose one tribe to research thoroughly. What did they live in? What did they eat? How did they travel? What ceremonies did they consider important? How did they dress? What kinds of art or music did they have? What games did the children play? After reading and researching this information, present what you have learned to your family. Be as creative as you can. You may want to build a replica of their home, their type of transportation, etc.

OTHER IDEAS/NOTES:

NORTH AMERICA: CURRENT EVENTS

Use the space below to record the articles you have found or the news that you have heard during your study of North America. Clip out the news articles and glue or paste them to a separate sheet of paper. Insert those pages after this page in your notebook.

Date of Newspaper or Radio/TV Broadcast	Name of Newspaper or News Station	Topic of News Item*
_____	_____	_____
_____	_____	_____
_____	_____	_____
_____	_____	_____
_____	_____	_____
_____	_____	_____
_____	_____	_____

* Examples: National currency, war, leadership, economics, government, environment, social issues, natural disasters (earthquakes, volcano eruptions)